My SEO Workbook

A Work guide on how to use words to make Search Engines send you customers, ready to open their wallets.

Thank you for your support. I'll see you in search

Copyright 2018
AKILAH THOMPKINS-ROBINSON

My SEO Workbook

ISBN 978-1-7335627-1-3

Copyright © 2018 by Online Boutique Source All rights reserved.

You are welcome to print a copy of this document for your personal use. Other than that, no part of this publication may be reproduced, stored, or transmitted in any form or by any means, electronic, mechanical, photocopying, recording, scanning, or otherwise, except as permitted under Section 107 or 108 of the 1976 United States Copyright Act, without the prior written permission of the author. Requests to the author and publisher for permission should be addressed to the following email: **info@onlineboutiquesource.com**

Limit of liability/disclaimer of warranty: While the publisher and author have used their best efforts in preparing this workbook, they make no representations or warranties with respect to the accuracy or completeness of the contents of this document and specifically disclaim any implied warranties of merchantability or fitness for particular purpose. No warranty may be created or extended by sales representatives, promoters, or written sales materials.

The advice and strategies contained herein may not be suitable for your situation. You should consult with a professional where appropriate. Neither the publisher nor author shall be liable for any loss of profit or any other commercial damages, including but not limited to special, incidental, consequential, or other damages. P.S. One or two of the links contained herein are affiliate links, meaning that at no extra cost to you, I may make a commission if you decide to purchase one of the linked items.

Copyright 2018

My SEQ Workbook

Table of Contents

Table of Contents 3
    Welcome to my corner of the online party 1

Chapter 1 **The Overview** 4
    Now let's talk about what is SEO. 5
    How to Get Found? 7
    What do search engines look for? 9

Chapter 2 **The Tools** 12
    Google Analytics (GA) 13
    Google Search Console 15
    Other SEO Tools 17
    Keyword Tools 17
    Content Research Tools 18
    Audit/Analysis Tools 18

Chapter 3 **Before you start** 20
    Knowing your business 22
    Researching your industry 22
    Knowing Your Customer 25
    Organizing your SEO Work 30

Chapter 4 **Is your site ready for SEO** 32
    Examining your Website 33
    URL Structure 34
    Site performance 35
    User Performance Metrics 36
    The Errors 38

Chapter 5 **Keywords are the Key** 40
    What are keywords? 42
    Keyword Research: R.A.C.E to #1 Method 43

Chapter 6 **Words Matter** 57

    How content and keywords mix 58
    What makes good SEO content? ... 59
    How to SEO the pages of your site . 60
    But, Am I just repeating yourself? 63
    Product Description Formula 64
    What really makes up your site, the code and tags 67

Chapter 7 **Blogs Glorious Blogs** 75
    Step 1: Choosing topics 78
    Step 2: Selecting Type 84
    STEP 3: Post it 98
    How Much Should I Write 101
    BUTTTTT I don't want to Blog 102

Chapter 8 **The Power of the Link** 106
    The power of the link 107
    Creating a beautiful link 108
    Internal links, aka Spread the Love 109
    External Links, aka Backlinks 112
    Some Dos and Don'ts of Backlinking 123

Chapter 9 **Keep this same SEO Energy** 126
    When will I see results from my SEO work? 127
    Why do things and Ranks Change 128
    Oh the Places you can SEO 130
    My 2019 SEO Predictions 132

The Journal Pages 135

The Planner Pages 160

Welcome to my corner of the online party

You've made the leap, took the step, and now you're ready to tackle the big bad beast they call SEO.

The good news is SEO isn't so bad, and as you work through the workbook, you'll see that SEO is a lot less scary than you think and you may already be doing great things that benefit your SEO. SEO uses many of the words we write every day on our sites, social media, or even words we speak to our clients; those same words can have Search Engines sending you thousands of clients and customers.

You're probably here because…

A) You're tired of depending on social media for every sale
B) You feel like you aren't getting anywhere on social media and you need another way to make your business work
C) Running ads is cool, but you really want to keep more of your profits in your pockets
D) You're tired of everyone talking about SEO but not showing you how to do it
E) Or your boss told you to read this

Whatever brought you here, WELCOME!!! I appreciate you taking the step with me, and I'm excited to lead you on your SEO journey.

This workbook is a little different than all of the other SEO books out there. I'm not just going to tell you how to do SEO, but we are going to work through it and do it. This book provides consistent exercises every step of the way to help you immediately put your new knowledge to work.

In this workbook, we're going to cover every step you need to go through to accomplish SEO on your site; you'll learn about keywords, analytics, backlinks and all of those other buzz words you hear about online.

You also learn a lot about writing, blogging that drives to sales, and most importantly using YOUR words to drive traffic.

This isn't your normal book on SEO; this is your Instructions, Workbook, Planner, Journal all in one. In addition to the lessons and exercises at the end of the book, I've given journal prompts that will help you shape your thoughts into blog posts and monthly action planner pages and various tracking sheets that are going to take you through your first year of SEO goodness.

A little bit about me and my little SEO journey, before we get started. My name is Akilah Thompkins-Robinson, I am the owner of Online Boutique Source, and I'm an online retail and SEO strategist.

And of course, today we are tapping way deep into the SEO portion.

I'm a Jersey girl, and I'd like to always bring that up because when you hear all of my references to malls and not pumping gas and a bunch of other Jersey-ish, you'll know where it's coming from. I'm a Jersey girl and most of all I'm a lover of free traffic. I've been doing SEO for real since 2013. I'm going to say for real because you know, sometimes you start things, but you aren't really doing it, yeah that was me around the year 2009.

I got serious about SEO in 2013 when I was a web designer. I wanted to find ways to not only get more traffic to my own sites but also to get more traffic to my client site.

Before that, I've had a total of 4 blogs, and each one of them had some type of SEO issue. I knew where some of my blogs went wrong, but for the others, I didn't figure it out until it was too late.

I'm definitely one of those "If I only knew then what I know now people" which is why I'm writing this book. After years of profiting from SEO traffic and working with clients to do the same, I've learned my way around this google thing, and I think every business owner should at least know the basics and write to attract clients.

I get tired of seeing businesses blog about themselves or some other fluffy topics that no one is searching for. I get tired of seeing people cry over Facebook ad payments like there is no other way to get traffic. I got tired of people asking, how do you do so well in your business and when I say "SEO or organic traffic" they run for the hills.

A Word about updates

If there is one thing, I've learned from 15 years in IT, it's that systems, applications, websites will change. The minute this book publishes someone is going to change something I've referenced in here and you are going wonder if the information is wrong. Well don't fret, I've created a resource site to put information about updates and I've added a few lists, videos, and other supplement information to help you with some of the technical steps in the book. Register for the resource site to get the updates and additional resources

http://onlineboutiquesource.com/seobookresources

So, this book along with my courses and membership is my way of helping business owners build a lasting, sustainable business, that helps their customers and increase their profit margins.

Note this book is for beginner - confused level business owners (meaning you know a bit but can't make it work). I'm not going to cover every single advanced SEO topic here. The goal of the book is to help you to get your SEO done. I follow the 80/20 rule here. I focus on the 80 % that is going to get you the greatest results very fast. The 20% you can get after you get traffic. If you're looking for the super advanced strategies like AMP, redirects, subdomain, etc. that'll be in the next book. If it's not here then it most likely not needed to get your first rankings, your first organic traffic, and make a big impact in your SEO marketing.

Chapter 1 The Overview

Ninety-five percent of the US Internet browsing population accesses search engines each month.

Now let's talk about what is SEO.

Search Engine Optimization (S.E.O) is adding content and making changes to your site so that it looks good to search engines so search engines will, in turn, send searchers (aka traffic) to your site.

When I say look good, I'm not referring your site logo, colors, or any other graphical elements. Looking good for search means that the words on your site are the ones search engines think will give the searcher the best information.

Google's (and every other search engine's) #1 goal is to keep people using their site to search for information. They've figured out that the best way to do that is by making sure when people use it, they get the best of the best and walk away with the answers they seek.

I say Google a lot in this book but just know when I say Google, I'm also referring to all search engines like Yahoo and Bing. Right now (2018) Google is King in the search industry, so we optimize heavily to meet their needs, in doing that we will do pretty well in the other search engines too

Another interesting stat

> "US population makes an average of 37 search engine visits per person per month."

People may tell you no one is searching but believe me people are still searching and at alarming rates. The other big difference in search traffic compared to social traffic is that when people are searching on search engines, they are usually ready to make the next move.

Think about it, if a pipe breaks in your house and you go to search for a plumber at the end of that search, you're ready to act. Either you'll hire a plumber or buy supplies to fix it yourself. You're ready to act on whatever information you find in your search. This is different than if someone sees a plumbing ad on social media. They may say to themselves "I need to remember that person for next time" but next time could be a while away, and they are more likely to forget all about the ad when the next time comes around. You can have the perfect audience, perfect location, and the perfect offers, but if the need isn't there, people won't act.

In the past, with SEO we spent a lot of time doing things to make sure that your code looks really good to Google on your site. Search engines, read HTML, PHP, CSS, and a bunch of other really technical code stuff, but your customer just reads the words you put on the screen, so we have to make sure they both count.

Another big part of what we do with SEO and content marketing is to make sure once people find you in their search, they want to actually be on your site and make their way to connect and purchase from your brand. I've found that a lot of SEO "gurus" will stress the importance of getting traffic but leave out the fact that you want that traffic to stick around and buy.

Here's one of the other reason's SEO is so darn important:

Aside from just getting found in search and getting traffic, SEO also helps to show your authority and credibility in your space. Customers are trained that the sites in the top of the search engines must be the biggest and best places for the service. By default, if you show up number #1 for something, they already have in their mind that you are at the top of your competition. Good content will not only help you get traffic but also establish your position in your industry (which can give you a boost on social too #win #win)

By the time you're done with this book you'll understand all of the marketing benefits and all of this SEO stuff too…

How to Get Found?

All search is not the same search. I'm not just talking about Google compared to social or Bing, but even within one search engine, a few different searches are going on when you hit that little magnifying glass.

In this workbook, I'll focus on the three main types of search. This is the big 80% that make up a majority of the results you see. I won't bore you with every single search because most people will never see it.

1. Text
2. Image
3. Video

When you search for something, often you'll see that three sections show up in the top listing. You may see a row of images, followed by a row of videos, and then text. The placement may change a bit based on which medium is most common for that particular search term.

These three things are actually three separate searches, so you could be number one in image searches and not number one in the text part, or you can be like number three in videos and number three on the texts.

A few years ago, I had a client who sewed blankets and pillow covers with popular cartoon characters. The text search for these characters was really competitive because she was competing with the creators, TV and movie mentions, major retailers and more; but the image search was wide open. I was able to quickly get her number one for images like Aladdin pillows and blankets and Doc McStuffins, beating out all of the major sites and heavy hitters, like Etsy.

The more you can optimize all three of these areas, the better your chances are of getting more people to see you.

Before you get too deep on how to rank for these things, I want you to take a little time to search for yourself in this next exercise.

My SEQ Workbook

EXERCISE

In this exercise take a minute to look for your site in Google's Search engine and see what results you get. What pages come up in text, images, and video. Search all three separately and make a list of what comes up.

[Hint: Enter site: **yoursite.com** in the search bar and it will give you a list of the pages google has listed for you]

Text →

Video →

Images →

What do search engines look for?

Search Engines decide what is going to be 1st, 2nd, or last in the search results using a weighted system called the **algorithm**. The algorithm is like a grading system where every site gets a grade, and the site's grades are compared to each other to determine their place in the search results. This comparison is called **ranking**. You may have heard this before, *"The algorithm changes and everyone's site go to hell"* (I'm joking, but not joking)

The grades are based on Ranking Factors. The **ranking factors** are 1000 little data points Google looks at to determine your rank.

The "fun" part is Google doesn't exactly tell us what all of the ranking factors are, or the exact grading process the algorithm uses. So, part of what we do here with SEO is to take what we know about what search engines like and try to get our sites the best grades we can.

What we do know is the ranking factors fall in 5 big categories, I call these the key to SEO:

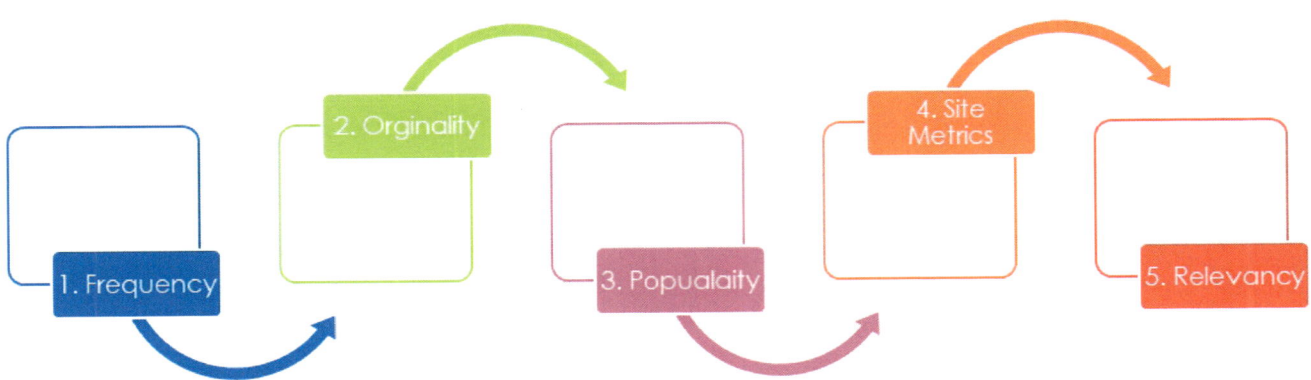

These keys are like a puzzle. When you put them all together, you unlock the magic to top ranking results. We're going to work through these in this book but here's a high overview to give you an idea of what your site needs to rank.

1. Frequency

Is your site updated pretty frequently? Are you adding content on a regular basis? Believe it or not, these things make a big difference to search engines. Search engines want to make sure they show the latest and greatest information, so they give an extra boost to sites that are frequently updated. The idea is if you are active on your site there is a good chance you keep your information accurate.

The frequency of your updates also let's search engines know how often they should look at your site for new information, and this is called **indexing**. If your site only gets updates every few weeks, it will take Google a much longer time to come back for new content. This will cause your rise in the search ranking to take a little longer than some of the other sites.

2. Originality

This is critical because Google hates duplicate content. When they're showing people resolve, they want to show them the best of the best, and they want to be able to show them different things. So, if you've got the same thing on your page as another site, even if that site is number one, that does not mean you're going to be number one, or you're going to be number two right there with them. Google is going to say, oh, well this is just a copy of what we already have, so we're not even going to show this at all. Originality is key. Even if you're thinking or doing a topic that people talked about before.

3. Relevancy

Relevancy is how close your content is to words or phrases users are actually searching for (keywords). For example, if I search for "best shampoo for red hair" and your site only says "best shampoo for black or blonde hair" your site will have less chances of showing up in my search results. Keywords are really, really important and we have a whole chapter on that later in the book.

4. Popularity

Popularity is the most forgotten piece of the SEO puzzle. In Google's mind, if your site is more popular, you must have the best information. So, when someone searches for a word or phrase, they are much more likely to get the top-ranking outcome, because the top-ranking site is the most popular. Our goal is making sure this word or phrase is on your site. This is the most difficult and skipped category because your popularity isn't measured by how many people visit your site or your social media numbers, popularity is how many people link to your site. A link from another site to yours is called a **backlink**. When I had my site Blogs Her Color, I gained a lot of backlinks because the blogs featured linked back to my site. I didn't know it at the time, but I was sitting on a backlink goldmine. We'll talk a lot about backlinks in this book but until then just know Google is not an island you have to build connections to it.

5. Site Metrics

Last but not least Google pays a lot of attention to how your site is performing and how well people are enjoying your site. **Site metrics** are technical things that people avoid like website code and sites speed, but it's also a bunch of other rank factors that are a lot easier to understand. Like how many pages someone visits on your sites, time on site, do they visit on page and leave or visit other pages. Site metrics are a little bit of everything you need to do to improve SEO. It is like your site platform like WordPress, Shopify, Wix or Weebly. Another thing that's really important is how fast your site is. There is not a lot you can do about the speed of your site, but especially if you're on WordPress, there's some things we do to slow down our sites. Like a lot of plugins, and large graphic files

> **SIDE NOTE:** New content doesn't only mean a blog post. All text on your site is new content to search engines. That means new products, services, testimonials, FAQs and anything else you type is helping your current status

can slow down your site. I won't get too technical in this book, but we'll talk about the things to avoid that impact your site metrics and how to improve on some of the user experience areas and have people excited to stay on your site longer.

That's a little bit about SEO. You may already have known some of these SEO tidbits, but I wanted to make sure I did a review to confirm you have a good sense of it. Now we can officially all start on the same page!

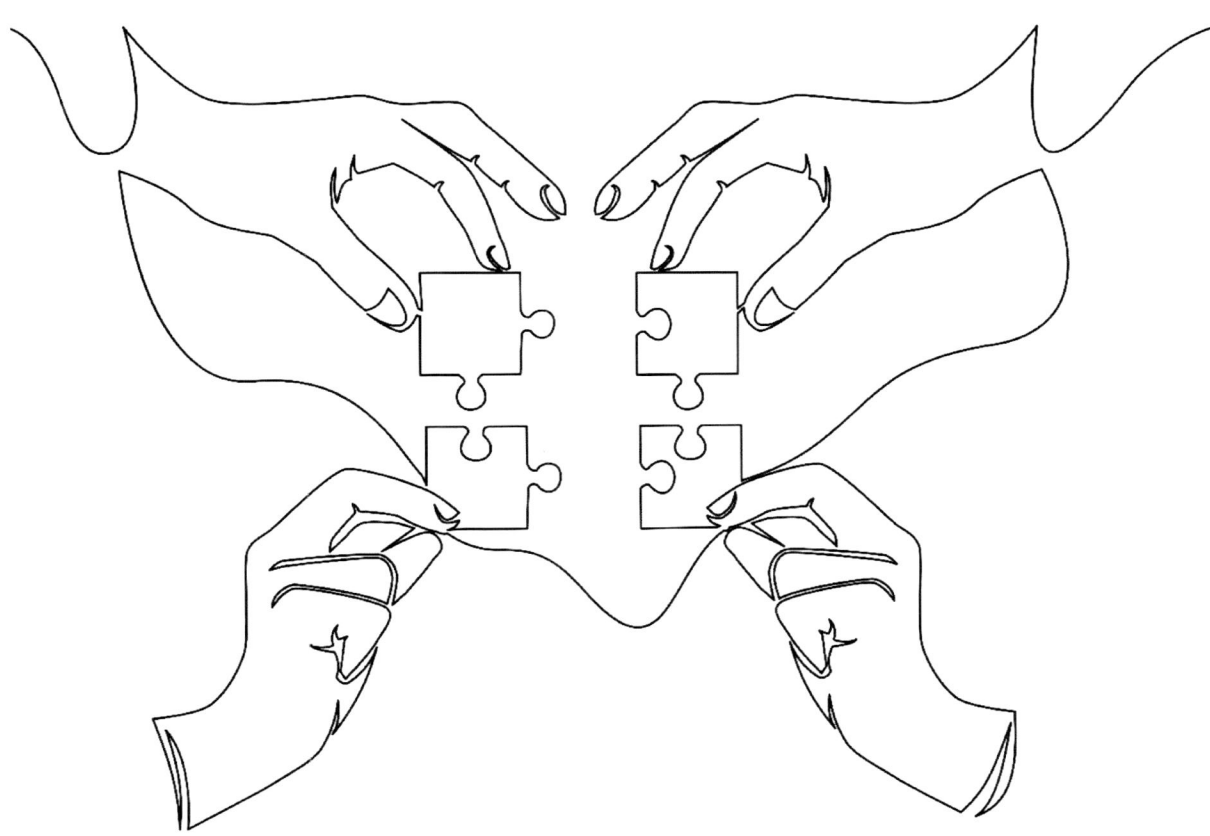

Chapter 2 **The Tools**

You can't build a house with out the proper tools

There are a lot of big fancy tools for SEO, like MOZ, SEMrush, Serpstat and AHref that you probably read about (and I'll talk about later). But unless you are running an SEO agency, you won't need all of that

The two most import tools are free. Yes, free

Google gives us 2 of the best tools for you to assess how you're doing in the search engines and how well your site can perform in the search rankings.

I call them the "look back" and "look forward" tools of SEO

Google Analytics (GA)

First is our "look back," Google Analytics. Google Analytics is a free online tool provided by Google which tracks all of the traffic coming to your site. Google analytics is one the most robust tools for gathering data and insight on who's visiting your site and what they are looking for.

To use GA, you have to install a small code on your site (visit the resource site for instructions) that enables Google to track your site visits.

Many people already use google analytics to see traffic on their site, but often overlook some of the deeper analytics that gives you an idea of how well you're doing. It also provides information on some of this site metrics and ranking factors I referenced to in Chapter 1.

I could write a whole book on all the data GA gives you, but for this book, I'm just going to focus on the things you need to help you with your SEO.

EXERCISE

Get Familiar with Google Analytics

For this exercise head over to Google Analytics to take a first look at your critical metrics. Write down your numbers we'll use them again later. (visit the resource site http://onlineboutiquesource.com/seobookresources for video completing this exercise)

Metrics to look for	Amounts
How many people have visited your site in the last 30 days, 90 days, and 1 year?	
What's are your average monthly visitors?	
What is the Bounce rate in the last 30 days?	
What is the average # of pages viewed per visit in the last 30 days?	
How many visits are coming from Google (this will be labeled as Organic on the list)	
What are the top 3 most visited on your site?	
What are top three traffic sources sending traffic to your site	

Copyright 2018

Google Search Console

Our next tool is Google Search Console (formerly known as Webmaster Tools). It is the 2nd critical Google tool you will need to work on your SEO. Just like Google Analytics it's free and installed using a shortcode. If you already have GA installed, you can use the same code in Search Console. (visit the resource site for instructions). While google analytics gives you a look back at what has happened on your site, Search Console gives you a peek into the future of what could happen.

Search Console shows you how the search engine currently sees your site, and how it is ranking it. Some of the important things you'll learn from Search Console is who is linking to you, what keywords you are ranking for, and what your top performing pages are. We use the Search Console Data throughout the SEO process to see how well we are doing and where we should focus our efforts to get maximum results the fastest.

The good news is if your site has been up and running for a while (even a few months) you most likely will have a lot of search analytics information that you aren't familiar with yet. In this next exercise, I want you to poke around Search Console and see what it says about your site. We'll be spending a lot of time in Google Search Console so don't skip this exercise, get to know search console. (visit the resource site for instructions)

My SEO Workbook

EXERCISE

Get Familiar with Google Search Console

For this exercise head over to Google Search Console to take a first look at your critical metrics. Write down your numbers we'll use them again later. (visit the resource site http://onlineboutiquesource.com/seobookresources for video completing this exercise)

Metrics to look for	Results
How many pages indexed? (this should be close to the number of pages your site has)	
Number of external links (sites linking from outside of your site)	
Top 10 Relevant Keywords you're ranking for (this is tricky at first because you may rank for keywords that have little to do with your business). These keywords won't hurt you, but they don't help either, so don't put these in your count)	
Top 5 pages you are ranking for (exclude pages like contact, privacy policy pages etc.)	

Metrics to look for	Results
Number of Keywords you are ranking for	
Number of internal links (links from one page on your site to another)	
Lowest 10 Relevant Keywords you're ranking for (this is tricky at first because you may rank for keywords that have little to do this your business. These keywords won't hurt you, but they don't help either, so don't put these in your count)	
Lowest 5 pages you are ranking for (exclude pages like contact, privacy policy pages etc.)	

Other SEO Tools

Aside from the main Google tools that we regularly use in the SEO process, there are several free and paid tools that we use from time to time. These tools aren't mandatory, but they make the SEO process a lot easier, and the information is more accurate than we would get if we tried to do it ourselves. Some of the tools give similar information so I've put them in 3 categories and you can pick and choose which you prefer. As we work through the chapters, I often reference my favorites, but I know they are not the only ones available for you.

Keyword Tools

We'll talk a lot about keyword research in Chapter 5; there are a few great tools to make the process easier. The main reasons to use keyword research tools is because they'll give you numbers and data to measure if a keyword is right for you or not and they'll also give you suggestions of other relevant keywords that you may not have thought of yet.

- *Long Tail Pro (longtailpro.com) $$*
  This is my keyword research tool of choice. It's paid services that measure the keyword volume, competition, and gives suggestions. They also keep track of the keywords you've researched in the past and have a few other tools that you can use to track how your site is doing for specific keywords. I've used this one for years because they stay up to date on ranking changes to ensure you have the most accurate information.
- *UBER Suggest (https://neilpatel.com/ubersuggest/)   FREE*
  SEO Guru Neil Patel created this tool. This is a great tool to get your feet wet and dabble a little in keyword research. This gives you Volume, Search trends, competition, and great little tips from Neil. The only issues I've found with the tool is you can't store and track past research, and the related keyword information is very limited.
- *Keywords Everywhere (Google Chrome Extension) FREE*
  Keywords Everywhere is a handy little extension that will give you information for keywords you search for. You have to use chrome for this tool, and the keyword information shows right up on your Google search page. The major downside I have to this tool is only certain keywords will show data. Keywords that aren't frequently

---

WHAT NO GOOGLE KEYWORD PLANNER!!!

You'll notice I didn't recommend the Google Keyword Planner in this section. Google keyword planner was a tool developed by Google to help people running PPC ads to research keywords to target. It was a great tool YEARS ago but in recent years, Google has made a lot of changes to make this only available to accounts running ads. When you sign up, you'll be asked for a credit card number and the accuracy of data depends on the amount of money you spend on ads. Also, Google keyword planner has never given you the competition score for keywords. This is important information for the SEO process. Because of these reasons, I've no longer recommend the tool and opted for the ones listed above.

updated won't have any available information.

Content Research Tools

We use these tools to help find topics that are going to bring us the best results. I'll share how to assess data too but trust me to use the tools manually. You can spend hours researching on your own and still miss some critical topics that can fast-track your rankings.

- **Answer the Public (answerthepublic.com) FREE**
  Answer the public gives you a really good list of the top questions asked about a specific keyword. This is a great tool to use if you're stumped for content ideas. The only downside is the search only works for more generic terms, and you may have to search for general keywords and mix in your more specific terms on your site. Currently, the tool is free. However, they have just introduced a paid version, so, they may limit some of the usages soon. My recommendation is to use the free as much as you can now.
- **BuzzSumo (https://buzzsumo.com/) $$$**
  I love BuzzSumo because it is one of the most robust tools to research what topics people are searching for and engaging with. In addition to researching keywords, you can also search by the website to see their most popular post and/or search social sites to see what content is being shared the most. The only downside is BuzzSumo is pretty pricey, I wouldn't recommend getting a subscription unless you are creating content for clients and can justify the ongoing cost. This tool is definitely on my 'really nice to have but not a must' list.
- **Google Trends (https://trends.google.com/trends) Free**
  This is another great tool from Google. Not as robust as our top 2 but still a good one to save in your favorites. Google trends gives you historical and current data on the topics people are searching for worldwide. This isn't as specific as keyword research, but this will give you the most information on what is important about that keyword. For example, when Megan and Prince Harry got married, Google Trends about the Royals were all over the charts.

Audit/Analysis Tools

We'll talk about SEO audits and how to see what needs to be optimized on your site in Chapter 4. The following tools will be your saving grace, if you prefer to have data run automatically, instead of manually. These tools are also the more advanced tools SEO pros use, so some of them have additional functionality we won't cover here in this book.

- **Serp Stat, SEM Rush, MOZ, AHRef $$**
  I lumped these together because they all do basically the same thing. They analyze your site to look for SEO errors and give some insight on the errors and ways to improve your ranks. The downside is they are a bit pricey and really built for the SEO pro-level. Trying out the limited free versions instead, are a good idea to play around with because it is information that is easily available.

  I personally use SEM Rush and SERP Stat in my business, Serp Stat gives the best Audit Reports because it is very thorough and easy to read and share with clients and SEM

Rush has some great tools for ongoing monitoring and comparison to compare where you are to your competition.

I recommend playing around with the free versions of each to determine your preference.

- **Minion (Google Chrome Extension) FREE**
  This is a newer tool find and thank GOD I found it. Until I found this tool, free SEO audits were nearly impossible and could take hours of work. Minion does a really nice single page analysis of any webpage your browser is on and tells you what possible SEO errors you have on the page. The only downside is you have to visit each page to get the errors for your site, but it's definitely better than the alternative of visiting pages and manually finding errors.

- **Yoast SEO Plugin (WordPress Plugin) FREE**
  This book isn't specific about using any platform, but I would be SEO trash if I didn't mention that every WordPress user should be using this. LOL. Yoast does a lot more than just an analysis for WordPress users. It provides the fields to input tags, does post and page SEO analysis, tracks internal links, creates sitemaps, and does on-site SEO tasks you'll see me mention in this book.

  The Yoast SEO Plugin is the Holy Grail of SEO plugins if you have a WordPress site. There are other SEO plugins, but YOAST has remained the best for the last 5-6 years, so just go for it.

Chapter 3 Before you start

"Check yourself before you wreck yourself" holds true for SEO too.

Before you get started with SEO, we have to talk about how well you know your business and customers. SEO is a strategy to drive traffic to your business but if it's the wrong traffic or the business isn't clear when they get there, then you won't be able to get the full benefit of all of this SEO stuff.

The greatest problems I find with businesses starting with SEO is, their keywords and content aren't relevant to what their audience is looking for.

You know how they say "attract people like bees to honey" well you have to know a little about your bees and make sure your honey is for them before anyone will be attracted to it. So, before we dig into how to do SEO let's talk about what you want people to find you for and the products you are selling.

In the next few sections I'm going to go through a few questions you should be able to answer about your business and customers. I'll also share a few ways to research all of this. I know you've probably taken a course with some type of target market or ICA spreadsheet, but I promise it's worth it to go through these with SEO in mind. Here's the BONUS good news -- the questions and answers will appear throughout this book, so consider it pre-work for the next chapters.

Let's get to know your business and customers

> **TIP:** An important part of research is to make sure you look at user generated content not brand generated content. Comments, reviews, forums, user groups, pin boards all fall under user generated content because it is created by actual customers and not driven by ads and brands. Brand generated content are FB pages, Websites, paid and sponsored ads, etc. Brand generated content is nice to look at but doesn't give you a true picture of what customers are looking for and thinking. It's heavily influenced by ad dollars and marketing. Think Go Daddy Super Bowl ads, Go Daddy isn't the greatest, but they gained popularity by running expensive ads. When you're researching what your customers want, make sure you're looking at actual customer data

Knowing your business

Knowing your business isn't as easy as it sounds. Most people look at their business from the position of what I built and what you intended for this to be, but in these exercises, I want you to step back and think about how other people see what you've built.

How do other people see your business, your services, and your industry?

SEO is all about showing up for what people are already looking for, so, as you go throughout this process, be careful not to stay stuck on what you think it should be, listen to how other people view your business.

Researching your industry

Research is a big part of this chapter, get ready to get your own Google on. Here are a few research strategies I would always recommend.

- **Predictive Search**
    Predictive search is that little drop down that appears in Google when you start typing in the search box and then Google tries to complete your sentence. A little annoying but don't ignore it, those words that are coming up are from the most commonly searched terms. Pinterest also has predictive search; in Pinterest, they show you common words at the top of the page under the search box. We'll use this again for our keyword research in chapter 5.

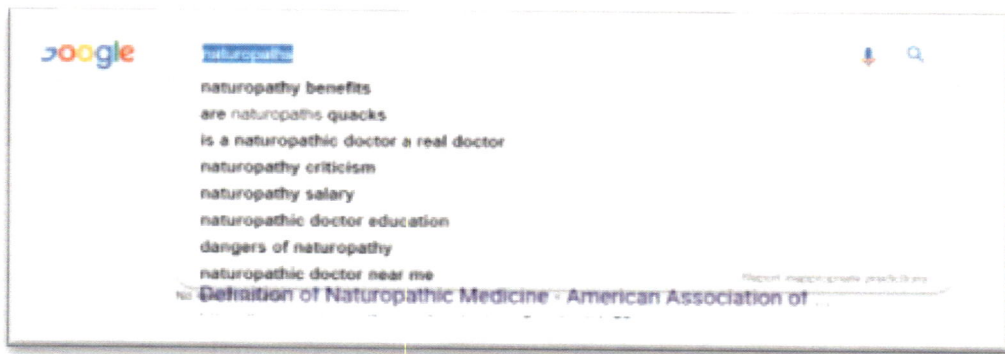

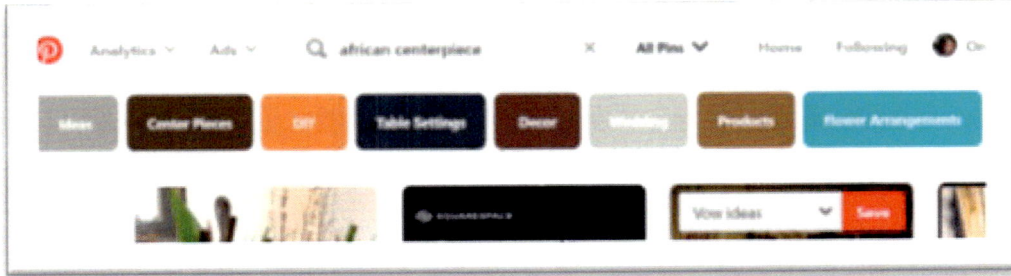

- **Pinterest Boards**
  Pinterest is still one of the most user-generated content and social platform. While more and more brands are creating boards, Pinterest is still created by users, and you can see how users are naming boards and the kind of pins they are putting together to give you a good idea of what users are thinking. **HINT: Check the name and profile of boards you are researching to ensure they are users and NOT brands**

- **Facebook Groups**
  FB Groups is another great user-generated curated space. A lot of people join Groups to learn and ask questions but, in this book, we join to research. Join groups where your ideal customer is and take some time to read through the type of questions people ask inside the group. See what things they post about that are bothering them (pain points) or helping them (wins). In most cases, if there is one-person brave enough to ask or share something publicly, there are 100s if not 1000s of people who have the same question. Resist the urge to ask a bunch of "what if" questions in these groups, feedback based on hypothetical situations aren't nearly as valuable as listening to what people say (or type) when they aren't prompted.

- **Answer the Public (and other trend sites)**
  Answer the Public, Google Trends, Buzzsumo, etc. are a few items that track and analyze trends of what people are looking and engaging with on various sites. Answer the Public and Google trends are free at the time of this writing, Buzzsumo has a little price but offers a nice free trial to get your initial research done. I'll talk more about these tools in the next chapter.

EXERCISE

Knowing your business

This section is less about what I write and more about you. After all, this is a WORKBOOK right! I can't tell you about your business, but I can give you this exercise to start researching the information you'll need to create content your customers and clients are looking for.

[Hint: Use some of the research tolls I've previously mentioned to answer the following questions.]

Questions	Answers
Describe using 10 words what you do?	
Describe using 10 words the results you help people get?	
What is your niche, industry or category of your business?	
If you were to look for your business title on Monster or Indeed what would the job title be?	
Look again at the above job titles and list 5 responsibilities of each role (that you meet in your business).	
List 3 (three) consistent problems a customer/client usually have before they reach out to you.	
What is your niche, industry or category of your business?	
What style or technique is your product or services?	

Knowing Your Customer

Next to knowing your business, knowing your customer is the 2nd most important thing you'll need for SEO. When we talk about knowing your customer, it's important to analyze them before they become your customer. What do they call themselves, what problems do they have before and after they buy your products, what is it about them that makes them different than anyone else?

For example, most people would see me and say I'm a female, African American, mother, wife, employed. But there is so much more to my story. What makes me different than any other female, African, American moms. To add, I'm also 5'1", I'm an older mom (I had my son at 36), I love and prefer having red hair, I travel a lot, and I'm a proud Jersey Girl :D

All of these unique, small things about me is important for when I start searching for products and solutions online. They also make a big difference in what kind of content and example I will find interesting and relate to.

EXERCISE	*Knowing your customer* *For this exercise, we're going to play a little game called "what makes it different" instead of the average "list their demographics." I want you to first list the initial demographic information under the column that says, "Your customer answers." The under the "what makes them different" column, I want you to then dig deeper to answers what makes your customer different than anyone else in the same category*

For example:

Category	Your customer's answers	What makes them different
Children	Yes, I'm a mother	I became a mother at an older age.

I'll give you a few prompts to get you started and some blank lines at the end to add your own categories:

Category	Your customer's answers	What makes them different
Marital Status		
Children		
Working status		
Where do they live		
What type of TV do they like		
What type of music do they listen too		

26 Copyright 2018

My SEO Workbook

What style of clothing do they prefer		
Where do they live (location)		
Where do they live (type of home)		
What kind of news do they follow		
Where do they go with friends		
What kind of work do they do?		

Need help with categories?

If you are having a little difficulty with creating your categories, use the below questions to brainstorm some ideas:

- Who are your ideal customers?
- How do they describe themselves?
- What are their goals?

Last but not least, in this section, another goal is for you to be really be able to describe the problem or problems your business solves.

"People search for businesses to solve a problem or meet the need they have, if you don't solve a problem then you don't have a business."

These last set of questions are to get you to think about problems you solve and how people would search for them:

- When do people use your products (time of year, an event in their life, etc.)?
- What result does someone get from your product or services?
- What are three ways they describe their problems?
- What are three ways they describe their solutions?
- Who would buy your products?
- What would a customer do with your products or service?
- What problem does your product or service solve?
- What are the first questions a potential customer asks that your product or service answers?
- What are recent headlines about your niche?

EXERCISE

Pulling it all together, fill in the blanks

Now that we know our business and our customer you should be able to complete the following statement. Consider this your Searchable elevator pitch. You want people to know what you do, who you help, how you help, and the results they should expect, all from a few words they put into a single search

[Hint: If you have multiple businesses or services, try to avoid using the same elevator pitch. Instead, complete a statement for each business or service.]

Finish this statement

I help _____ (who do you help) to _____ (what service do you provide) so that they can _____ (what result do you help with) so they don't have to _____ (benefit of your service)

Here's is an example:

I help **Women business owners** (who do you help) to get **found on search engines** (what service do you provide) so that they can **reach more customers and get more sales** (what result do you help with) so they don't have to **spend money on ads** (benefit of your service)

Organizing your SEO Work

Now that we've gotten the foundation stuff out the way lets jump into ways to make your rankings happen. You're probably worried that this ranking stuff is a lot. I'm not going to lie, there are a number of steps, but we've got it down to a science, and I'm sharing that science here with you!!

When my team and I start with a new client, we pull out "The Ranking Checklist." This is a handy list of mandatory steps we need to complete, to make sure a client's SEO is in tip-top shape. To make this process just as simple for you we'll be using the same checklist. At the end of each chapters there will be a copy of the checklist and I'll check off the steps we've learned in that chapter.

This will help stay on track to make sure all of the important task gets done and if you get a little off track along the way you can use the checklist to let you know where to refer back to.

TIP: When we're working on a client's site, we put dates next to each task in the Ranking checklist, this helps to set a timeline and keep the whole team on track with the work we're doing. I've added an electronic version of the checklist in the resource section so that you can use it again and again.]

The Ranking Checklist

1) **Initial site checks**
   - ☐ Confirm Google analytics access (Chapter 2)
   - ☐ Confirm Google search console (Chapter 2)
   - ☐ Get Current Metrics (Chapter 2)
   - ☐ Do initial site readiness checks (Chapter 4)
     - ☐ 404 errors
     - ☐ Address URL issues
     - ☐ Blank descriptions
     - ☐ Dupliccte content
     - ☐ Broken links
     - ☐ Blank alt tags

2) **Complete keyword research (Chapter 5)**
   - ☐ Round Up- Create list of potential keywords
   - ☐ Analyze- Check volume and competition for keywords
   - ☐ Connect- Create a potential list of topics and categories
   - ☐ Engage- Test your words out in post and on social
   - ☐ Select 5-10 focus keywords

3) **Update Content on site**
   - ☐ Add keywords to pages on your site (Chapter 6)
   - ☐ Find Update images (Chapter 6)
   - ☐ Update page tags, descriptions, headings, images, etc. (Chapter 6)
   - ☐ Choose SEO friendly topics (Chapter 7)
   - ☐ Choose blog post types you like (Chapter 7)
   - ☐ Write 5-10 blog post (Chapter 7)

4) **Internal inks (Chapter 8)**
   - ☐ Identify pages without links
   - ☐ Identify pages to link to on your site
   - ☐ Create internal links

5) **External Linking (Chapter 8)**
   - ☐ Find link building opportunities
   - ☐ Fid group to collaborate with
   - ☐ Monitor incoming links

6) **Wrap up and ongoing (Chapter 9)**
   - ☐ Schedule future blog post
   - ☐ Pitch link building opportunities
   - ☐ Update target keywords
   - ☐ Complete Monthly Look back and plan ahead
   - ☐ Monthly 2-4 blog post with internal link
   - ☐ Monthly 5-10 backlinks

Chapter 4 Is your site ready for SEO

"He who is not in readiness today, will be less prepared tomorrow"- Marcus Valerius Martialis

We talk a bit about Site Fitness in 5 key areas of SEO in chapter 1. Site fitness digs into site metrics, errors, and structure which can get a bit technical, but you don't need to know code or fancy systems to improve your site metrics. The important thing is to make sure your site has a solid foundation, and you're not doing anything that will cause any errors for search engines. In this chapter, I want to give you an overview of things you should focus on to make sure you've had this part covered.

The five keys that we referenced in chapter 1, isn't in order of importance to search engines. Instead, I put them in an implementation order. It's to give you an idea of which key you should focus on and when to build your sites SEO successfully.

For example, popularity is really important to Google it's one of the major things you need to get found in the search rankings, but you would not implement backlink strategies to drive popularity until after you've at least looked at your site set-up your site metrics to ensure there are no issues that will drop your rankings. You'll see the next five chapters are in order of how you should be implementing them, not the order of importance in Google Writing rankings.

The other advantage of working on your site metrics in this order is for you to gain traction faster in the search engines. You are first creating a solid foundation and then building on top of that. Google will begin searching your site as you add content and rank you a lot faster than if you focus on other areas first.

Examining your Website

Most websites are built on a content management system (CMS) these days. These systems like WordPress, Squarespace, etc. makes it easy for you to create sites without knowing how to code. Even web designers often use a CMS as their base and then customize the code on top of it.

The important thing you need to know about platforms is discovering which platform is your website built on.

I've mentioned before Search engines only read text and code; they see all of the HTML and CSS that makes up your site. Unless you are coding your own site (don't worry no one really does that anymore), you are depending on the platform you use to write good codes, that makes it easier for search engines to find what's important on your site.

Best Platforms: WordPress, Shopify, Squarespace
Worst Platforms: Wix, Weebly, or using Lead Pages for your site

People hate to hear this part, but it's really important that we understand how your platform affects your site. WordPress for example was built with bloggers in mind, and for the most part, WordPress has very clean codes or clean as you can get codes.

NOTE: When a platform or your web designer says they have SEO, or they've built SEO into your site, that does NOT mean they've done all of the work, and it will instantly rank. What that usually means is they have set up fields for you to put keywords and tags in which makes it easier for you to understand where to place them. We'll talk about this more in chapter 6.

URL Structure

The URL is the address for your site. Http://www.yoursite.com/page. This URL is very important to how search engines categorize pages of your site. First, the URL is very specific www.yoursite.com is different than yoursite.com. Same as if your site has HTTP or HTTPS, these are two different URLs.

Here's a list of URL do's and don'ts

- Do ensure the URL is clear English www.yoursite.com/blogtitle is much better than www.yoursite.com/p12a45e

- Do ensure your URL starts with your site name, not an extension for your platforms like Wix or Weebly. Example yoursite.wix.com is really pointing to the Wix site, not your site. If you are using a platform that gives you an extension domain, go ahead and buy your own domain. It's important!

- Don't separate your site into multiple domains. For example, if you have a store and a blog, they should be the same URL. Google will see yoursiteblog.com and yoursitestore.com as 2 different sites. This will be important when we talk about internal links and link juice.

- Don't use subdomains if you want the content to be searchable. A subdomain is another way of separating sections of your site, blog.yoursite.com or store.yoursite.com. It is similar to separating site names, and search engines will not attribute these to being one site as we need it to be.

- Don't sweat the .com stuff (this is a bit of good news), although I like .com because it's easier for users to remember, having a different extension like .co, .net or .info won't hurt your sites SEO. As long as the site is consistent, search engines won't penalize your extension. The only extensions that are treated a little differently are .gov, .edu., some .orgs, and sex-related extensions. Sites ending in .gov, .edu, and .orgs are sometimes seen as more official sites and have a slight advantage in the ranks, and of course, sex extensions are excluded from more general search results.

Site performance

Even if you are on a good platform, there are a few key metrics that can cause issues with your site. For example, having a really slow site or having pages that search engines can't find.

Look at your site and make sure there aren't any big issues before moving forward

Technical Performance Metrics

I'm only going to talk about this at a very high level in this book because like I've stated before, this is not going to be a very technical book. The goal of this section is to eliminate any major issues on your site and to make sure you have a general understanding of the critical parts of SEO.

This cannot be skipped! It's extremely important to know and analyze these things. The reason is that, immense issues can affect how fast and how well your site is going to perform.

- **Site speed**
  Site speed (technical metric), is the measurement of how long it takes your site to load. There are a lot of things that affect your site speed, but the big ones are platform, plugins (if you're using WordPress), the number of images, etc. I use a tool called **GTmetrix** to measure how well my site is performing. It's a free site that measures your site speed by providing you a lot of measurements.

- **Responsiveness (aka is your site is mobile-friendly)**
  This is a simple yes or no metric, either your site is good on mobile, or it's not. The good news is that currently in 2018, most platforms automatically give you a mobile-friendly site, especially if you're on WordPress. Google has a nice checker that will help you if your site is responsive or not.
  https://search.google.com/test/mobile-friendly
  Not only is responsiveness important for Google, but also a lot more people are looking and doing things on mobile now. You want it to be as mobile-friendly as possible, check your content on your phone regularly because if it's hard to see or read you'll lose people.

  NOTE: Stay away from sites that do what they call M sites. These are special sites that have m.yoursite.com. This M is an older way that web platforms were using to make the site accessible on mobile by creating a 2nd site just for mobile. These sites are bad for SEO because Google sees them as a separate site from your website, which splits all of the traffic and metrics we'll talk about below. If your URL starts with **M**, when you view it on mobile phone, talk to your web company immediately.

- **Secured Site (HTTPS)**
  A site with HTTPS means that there is a secure SSL certificate on your site and server. This is an extra layer of protection for your visitors and is especially important if you have an e-commerce site or forms where you collect information (this does not include email forms). Right now, HTTPS is not mandatory, but Google does give a little more preference to secure sites and has mentioned making it mandatory. If your site is currently HTTP and you want to move to HTTPS, contact your hosting service about

applying an SSL certificate. If you're going to do it, I strongly recommend doing that before you do a lot of SEO work,

- **Site Crawl**
  Crawling your site is when Search Engines find your site and visit each of your pages. I like to imagine little spider bots jumping from page to page scanning all of your content like that screen in the minority report. This scan is called indexing which is the most important thing for your SEO because, this is how and when search engines figure out what's on your site so that they can rank it. This site crawl usually happens automatically even if you aren't working on your SEO, but there are some rare occasions when there are indexing or crawl error. If this happens, work with your web designers or host to determine what issues need to be address. On the flip side, you can also help Google to crawl your site faster. This is available in Google Search Console where you can submit a sitemap and ask Google to help see all of your site. Lastly, adding content frequently and having links between pages makes it easier for search engines to crawl your site.

User Performance Metrics

This is how well your site is doing with visitors and how much time they are spending with your content. The good news is, this is one of the areas you have the most control over and can easily fix with changes to your content and structure. We'll talk about how to improve these metrics a lot in the next few chapters, but in this chapter, I want to give an overview of metrics we're looking for and how Google measures them

In the earlier chapters, I talked about ranking factors which are items search engines grade your site on, to determine where it will rank in search results. The content on your site is a big portion of these ranking factors, but there are also some ranking factors that are driven by how well and how long people interact with your sites, that's why I call these your user performance metrics. Refer back to chapter 2 where we talked tools such as Google analytics and Google search console. These tools will help you to measure many of these metrics and tell you how they're doing. In the upcoming content chapters, I'll give you tips on how to improve these metrics, but for now, I just want you to be familiar with what they are and how they impact your ranking.

- **Time on site**
  Google measures the average time someone spends on your site. This includes the average time someone is on a page, and those ranking factors are considered in whether or not your site is really providing value and is a good resource for searches.

- **Pages visited**
  Google tracks the average number of pages someone visits on your site. This includes the time and spent on your site and how many different pages are they flipping through. This is where it pays off the most to have a Blog because people are likely to click through a few posts and increase this visitation number.

- **Return visits to your site**
  Google also tracks how often someone returns to your site in an average number of days. This is another indicator of your value if the same person is returning to your

site. The returning number is measured by returns to your site and returns to the individual pages.

- **Bounce rate**
  This is a big one people talk about all of the time. The Bounce rate is the percentage people visit your site and then leave without going to another page first. The idea here is if people come to your site and leave quickly then your site did not give the information they were looking for. This is very important for organic search engine traffic because their goal is to give the best results when someone searches. If visitors visit your site and immediately leave, this is a sign to Google that the page did not have the information they were looking for.

- **Click-through rate**
  A click-through rate is how many times customers see your site on the search results page and click to visit. This is a similar logic behind bounce rate because search engines want to give people the best results. If your page is on a results page with 5-10 other sites and people chose other sites over yours, eventually the search engine will move those up the ranks. If you've got a business that is on page one, but it's a not enticing enough to drive traffic and increase the need for customers to click, you'll eventually be ranked down to page two or page three! Why? Because Google's going to give someone else that number one spot. We'll talk about this more in-depth but click through rate is very important to consider.

These are your top User performance metrics and as you can see many of the metrics are based on how users interact with your site and how much they consume your content. In the next few content chapters I refer to these metrics a lot, and I'll highlight the task we'll complete that will affect these metrics.

The Errors

Now let's jump into the LAST part of our Site Fitness check, the errors. The Errors aren't red flags or alerts that Google will tell you, but they are things that occur on your site that will affect how search engines see all of your content and how it indexes your site. Now that you understand a little about what search engines are looking for and how they measure your site, the errors are going to make a lot more sense.

The bad news is Google won't show you these errors in their tools. It's a little time consuming, but you can manually check your site, or use paid tools like SEMRush, Serp Stat or MOZ to run a site audit.

- **404 Errors**

  You may have seen these before as you've been surfing the internet. This is when someone visits a page on your site that doesn't exist. This can happen if someone mistype a page name, the link is incorrect or, most common way a link is clicked, and it is no longer there.

  Have you ever changed a page name or deleted a page on your site? If you have, you may have created a 404 error. When changing page names or deleting pages, it's important that you make sure any pages linking to the page are also changed.

- **Address URL Issues**

  We talked about creating readable names for your pages, earlier in the chapter. Another concern is, too long or too Short address URLs can cause an issue as well. A good rule is to keep the length of characters after the site name between 5-20 characters.

- **Blank Descriptions**

  We'll talk about page descriptions and tags more in the next chapter, but for this chapter, it's important to know this is a flag that will show up if you run an SEO audit. The page description is the little blurb that you see under the page name in the search listing. This description is important for a few reasons. It tells Google what the page is about and what to expect, and it also gives searchers a little preview. You can set your page description using the SEO fields provided in most CMS platforms.

  [Tip: if you search "site:yoursitename.com" in google it will show you all of the pages it has indexed for your site, and you can see which have the right descriptions.]

- **Duplicate Content**

  This fits with one of the 5 keys to SEO we discussed earlier, originality. This is also an important error to look out for on your own site. Even if you have similar or the same items on multiple pages of your site, for example, the same dress in red and green, you want to avoid using the same name and/or description. Try to mix it up, so this isn't seen as duplicate content.

- **Broken Links**
  This is similar to the 404 error, except this error is for the hyperlink on your page that's linking to the page that is no longer there. Broken links can be links to other pages on your site and links to pages on external sites. This is a little more difficult to find manually, but it's a good idea to check links on your site regularly and make sure they are still working and pointing to valid pages.

  [TIP: if you are changing a page on your site you can make a 301 redirect to the new page, which will automatically send clicks to the new location and avoid broken link issues. Use this solution sparingly, as Google is not a fan of a lot of redirects.]

- **Blank Alt Tags**
  Alt Tags are the tags that are attached to images. They give search engines an idea of what the picture is showing and provides some text if the image doesn't appear. I'll talk about this again in content, but this is a key area where many miss the SEO advantage.

These are just some of the top errors to look out for on your site. You can find many lists of tops errors online. The Yoast Plugin gives a nice Red Amber Green rating for pages that are based on many of these errors.

A lot of the errors can be avoided as your creating and adding content to your site. If you've had your site for a while, it may be a good idea to have an audit run and fix a few errors at a time. These errors are a ot of little things that can make a big difference in how well your site is optimized.

The Ranking Checklist

1) **Initial site checks**
   - ✓ Confirm Google analytics access (Chapter 2)
   - ✓ Confirm Google search console (Chapter 2)
   - ✓ Get Current Metrics (Chapter 2)
   - ✓ Do initial site readiness checks (Chapter 4)
     - ✓ 404 errors
     - ✓ Address URL issues
     - ✓ Blank descriptions
     - ✓ Duplicate content
     - ✓ Broken links
     - ✓ Blank alt tags

2) **Complete keyword research (Chapter 5)**
   - ☐ Round Up- Create list of potential keywords
   - ☐ Analyze- Check volume and competition for keywords
   - ☐ Connect- Create a potential list of topics and categories
   - ☐ Engage- Test your words out in post and on social
   - ☐ Select 5-10 focus keywords

3) **Update Content on site**
   - ☐ Add keywords to pages on your site (Chapter 6)
   - ☐ Find Update images (Chapter 6)
   - ☐ Update page tags, descriptions, headings, images, etc. (Chapter 6)
   - ☐ Choose SEO friendly topics (Chapter 7)
   - ☐ Choose blog post types you like (Chapter 7)
   - ☐ Write 5-10 blog post (Chapter 7)

4) **Internal inks (Chapter 8)**
   - ☐ Identify pages without links
   - ☐ Identify pages to link to on your site
   - ☐ Create internal links

5) **External Linking (Chapter 8)**
   - ☐ Find link building opportunities
   - ☐ Fid group to collaborate with
   - ☐ Monitor incoming links

6) **Wrap up and ongoing (Chapter 9)**
   - ☐ Schedule future blog post
   - ☐ Pitch link building opportunities
   - ☐ Update target keywords
   - ☐ Complete Monthly Look back and plan ahead
   - ☐ Monthly 2-4 blog post with internal link
   - ☐ Monthly 5-10 backlinks

Chapter 5 **Keywords are the Key**

You want people to know what you do before they even know who you are

Most people hear SEO, and they automatically jump into "I need the right keywords." Keywords are the most popular part of SEO, but they are also the most misunderstood. In this chapter we'll break down everything you need to know about keywords and come out the other end with a list of keywords that are perfect for your business.

What are keywords?

Keywords are words or phrases that searchers put in the search the search box. It's how they describe the item their looking for and how they hope websites will have the answers list on their site.

A keyword can be one word, a phrase, or a group of words.

>Example:
>
>Dress = keyword
>
>Black Dress= Keyword
>
>Black Prom Dress= Keyword
>
>Where to buy a black dress for prom= Keyword

That's right all of these falls under the definition of keywords. If you search all of these in Google right now, you'll find they all have different search results come up on page one.

Keywords fall into two categories short tail and long tail
Short Tail Keywords- These are just simple keywords one or 2 words (spoiler alert: these are the hardest to rank for and get the worst traffic)

Example: Dress, black dress, prom dress

Long Tail Keywords- These are more specific keyword 3 words or more, they usually add more description or further define what the searcher wants to do with the keyword

Examples: Black prom dress, pretty prom dress, where to find prom dress

A good SEO Keyword also known as a **"Golden Keyword"** isn't just the words and phrase that people type in the search box but it's also the keywords where there is a good number of people searching for them, and the competition is low enough that you have a good chance of ranking pretty easily. We find these keywords by doing keyword research. Pat Flynn calls research keyword research panning for gold hence the name "Golden Keywords."

In this chapter, we'll cover the R.A.C.E Keyword Research method I use to separate the golden keywords from the regular bunch.

Getting in the Keyword Games

I compare keywords to a track meet; there are dozens of races you can run at a track meet; the 100m, hurdles, 4x4, etc. Each race has its own set of racers, and you can win each race that you are in. Search Engines are the same way keywords are races, and you have billions of chances to win. Consider this the 'Keyword Games'

Now the bad news *(I promise it's not that bad)*
The bad news is all keywords are not the best for you and they won't help your business and bring you traffic.

Just like all track races are not the best to run in. I cringe when people say "I show up number one for my name." Being #1 for your names may sound nice and fun but most people aren't searching for your name, so it'll be one of those races you can win, but it doesn't have a great prize. Our goal is to get you in the right races where the prize is nice, and you have a good chance of winning.

Keyword Research: R.A.C.E to #1 Method

I've got a four-step formula for getting to your golden keyword; I call it the R.A.C.E keywords research method. Racing through your keyword research will take you from a bunch of random keywords to the keywords just right for driving traffic and sales to your website. I'll give you an overview of the process here, and then we'll break it down with the worksheets

The process is like a funnel or raceway, you'll have a bunch of keywords at the start, and by the finish, there are only a few winners.

My SEQ Workbook

Round Up your Keywords
- This is when you make list of possible keywords your want to start with, we call them seed keywords. These are the keywords you are probably thinking of right now. What is your business, who are your customers, what do you sell? All of these can be seed keywords.

Analyze Keywords
- Here's where a lot of the keyword tools will come in handy, we use the tools to analyze how many people are looking for this keyword (volume) and how many other sites are in the race for this keyword competition. Most keyword Tools will also give you other related keywords that you can add to your round up list

Connect
- Connect your keywords back to your business is so important. I often seen people come out with perfect keyword that isn't a perfect for their business. It's important to make sure the keyword fits your business and you can write about it. In this step we test it out to make sure a keyword is golden for you and your customer

Engage
- This last step takes right into the next chapter. Start using your keywords to engage with your potential audience. Don't wait until you write a dozen blog post and update your site, start using it now. In this step you can start usig your keyword in social media and any current touch points you have with customers. See how followers like and resonate with the keyords you'll be using.

Round-Up your Keywords

Keywords start out as just ideas. Right now you probably have some idea of keywords you want to be number one for, write them down they are **seed keywords**. Seed Keywords are the words you'll start with and through research find other words that fit. In the Round-up stage, we start to list of the keywords we want to considers and do some targeted research to "round up" additional keywords that could work for us.

Don't just start with the keywords in your head; there are several ways to research and create a really thorough keywords list. I'm going to list some great ways to get seed keywords

1. <u>Answering questions</u>- go back to the questions I asked you in chapter 3 about your business and your customer. You may not have realized it, but the answers you gave in that chapter are also keywords people could use to find you
2. <u>Words you're already ranking for</u>- in Chapter 4 we looked at words you're already ranking for in Google Search Console use this RACE method to see if those could be golden keywords and perhaps you need to use them more or write more about them to increase your rank.
3. <u>Words used on social</u>- this is another good time to revisit all of the research we've done, what words come up a lot on sites, social media, groups, etc.
4. <u>Words your competitors are using</u>- don't ignore the fact that your competitors are speaking your customer's language too, the words they are using could help you find your golden keywords too.

TIP: If you use a tool like SEMrush or Buzzsumo you can research Competitors sites just like you do your own and get some valuable words

5. <u>Industry words</u>- these are the words that are like your industry jargon. SEO, for example, is an industry word. Look at what words are around your industry, about your industry, different things that when people are starting to learn about what you do or sell, they can start looking it up. More example: products like peplum blouse peplum is more of an industry fashion word people would know unless someone told them or mentioned it somewhere. Funnels or sales funnels, those are actually industry keywords.

6. <u>Predictive search</u>. We used this Chapter 3 for our research; now we are going to use this to help round up some keyword. This is very common in Google and in Pinterest. I love both. Online predictive search is when you go to put in a word or two words, and Google tries to answer your question or, in Pinterest, they give you additional words that are associated. That's called predictive search, and those words are actually the most searched-for words that are accompanying whatever it is you put in.

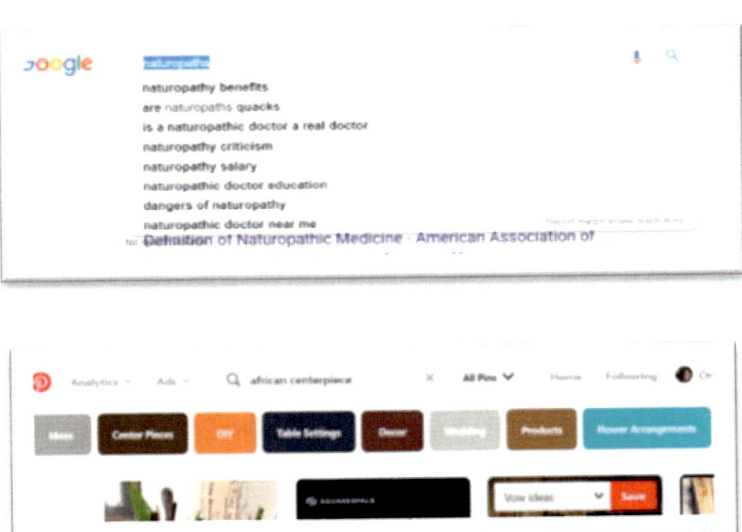

Example: If I started Googling crochet red or crochet hair, and it starts popping up red hair or how to install or how to braid, those are the words that people are usually searching with, searching for, along with the first couple of words that I put in. It's a good idea to take some of those initial seed keywords and put them in and see what kind of predictive search keywords you can get in addition to them.

7. Modifiers. Modifiers are words that you can put both in front of or in the back of your keywords, your seed keywords, to make them a little bit more long-tailed keywords enhances its meaning. Modifiers could be things like best of the top mistakes people ... mistakes made ... list of modifiers. Modifiers can and details or more of the intent of the search.

Modifiers Ideas:

- Location (in …)
- Size
- Color
- add limits (under $100, over $5000)
- generalization type (punk, grunge, hippie, millennials)

- Help with…
- Cheapest
- Smallest
- Biggest
- Lightest
- Fastest
- Introduction of
- Top (ranking)
- Reviews
- Information

- women
- men
- kids
- teens
- adults
- students
- Get
- Buy
- Purchase
- Compare

- Resources
- How to
- Samples
- Examples
- Plans
- Ideas
- Tips
- Tutorial
- find
- Best

8. Synonyms. Synonyms are one of my favorite ways of finding a good keyword. Synonyms are words that mean the same as the words you already have. They could be the same as seed keywords or as your industry words, so, yes, just like they do in the dictionary, you could have synonyms. Those synonyms could also be considered keywords.

When I was starting online boutique stores, I had a choice. I could do online retail, online stores, E-commerce, and online boutique, which is a synonym of E-commerce; once I did my research in the next step, I found that online boutique was the one that was well searched for and had the least amount of competition, and became my first golden keyword.

My SEO Workbook

EXERCISE

Round-Up Exercise

This Exercise is pretty simple. I want to help you try out every Round-up activity I tell you about in this chapter. Don't go overboard collecting a billion keywords or spending months on this step. Instead, limit yourself. In the sheet below list no more than 10 keywords per activity. Some of the activities you'll find more than 10 but to for now just stick to 10 that best suit your audience.

Words you're thinking of:	Answering Questions:	Words you're already ranking for	Words from Social Media
1	1	1	1
2	2	2	2
3	3	3	3
4	4	4	4
5	5	5	5
6	6	6	6
7	7	7	7
8	8	8	8
9	9	9	9
10	10	10	10

My SEO Workbook

Words your Competitors use	Industry Words	Predictive Search	Modifiers
1	1	1	1
2	2	2	2
3	3	3	3
4	4	4	4
5	5	5	5
6	6	6	6
7	7	7	7
8	8	8	8
9	9	9	9
10	10	10	10

HINT: some of these may overlap. You may get some that are answers to your questions and industry words. That can definitely happen if you have duplicates on your list. You only need one seed keyword list, so just make one.

Analyze

Now that we've rounded up a bunch of good seed keywords the next thing we're going to talk about is analyzing those Keywords (running the numbers).

In this step, you are getting the data behind those keywords we rounded up and running the numbers for the keywords you list.

You can have what looks like an amazing keyword but if the numbers tell up no one is searching it, or the competition is too much it's not a good keyword to move forward with

This is where some of the tools that we discussed in Chapter 2 will come in handy. I use a tool called LongTailPro, and so I am going to recommend that. It's a little bit of additional cost, but believe me, it's so worth it even if you just use the trial for a couple of days to get the initial work done.

Other tools you can use are UberSuggest or Keywords Everywhere, these do some of those things as the LongTailPro, just not as nicely packaged.

When doing Keyword Analysis, we look at two specific metrics:

Search Volume

This is the average number of searches for the specific term each month. You'll need to use one of the free or paid tools I recommend to find this number. Unfortunately, it is not publicly listed anywhere (I don't recommend Google Keyword planner for this)

You'll find this number within a few 100 of the actual number.

Competition Scores

This number will give you an idea of how many other sites are also trying to rank for the same keyword and how successful they are at it. Each tool as a slightly different name and way of showing the score but the idea is still the same to want the lowest score possible.

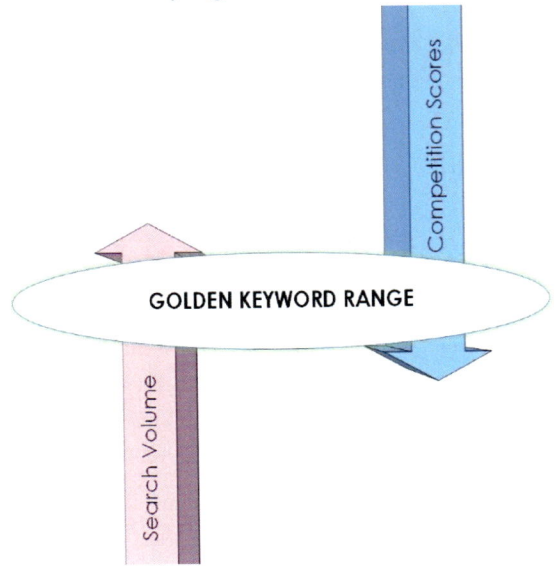

The goal of looking at the two numbers is you want keywords with the decent search volume and lower completion. Most like this will not be the keywords with millions or 100,000s searches; the golden range is usually lower around 1000-50,000 searched

Start with the low hanging fruit...
Depending on your site, if you're just getting started with SEO, you want to keep your search volume very

low and go for the least competitive. As your SEO rankings grow, you will be able to go after a few more competitive words.

The volume and competitiveness score are like SEO scales. If it's really high volume, but the competitiveness is high, it's really a good volume, but the competitiveness is high, you won't win that race. If the competition is low, but no one's looking for it, then you don't even want to be in that race. Keep that in mind when you're doing, when you're running your numbers and doing those keyword research.

A lot of people say, "Well, this keyword has a million searches or 60,000 searches." These numbers are nice, but the competition is usually harder for those higher volumes. It'll be much hard to compete for those words and take longer to get your first ranks. Whereas, if you go for the lower numbers first win those and then look at higher the number those initial ranks will help you to do better with the harder keywords.

Example Search Ranges:

Site Age and Size	Recommended Search Volumes
Small or Newer Site	100-5000
Mid-Size Site or more than 1 year with content with some organic traffic coming to your site	5,000-20,000
Larger site or consistently creating content a few years	20,000-100,000

Don't be discouraged is the search volumes seem low, remember it's just one keyword the combination of all the keywords on your site will make up your overall traffic. Each Keyword is just one of the many races you'll be in.

Getting the Competition Score

I highly recommend using a tool to determine your score they do a lot of the work for you, but it's a good idea to know what are the factors that make a keyword more competitive and how to look for it manually too.

To manually assess the keyword

- Step 1 Search for the keyword in Google (use incognito search if you are in chrome)
- Step 2: Look at the listings on the first 2 pages (about 15-20 top listings) answer the following for each listing
    - Are there big-name stores and sites and businesses? Is it like Amazon or CNN or Fortune Magazine? Those are going to be more competitive and harder to beat out. You want to look for if it's like a blog or just another site.

- Is the site using the exact keyword you searched for or is it part of a phrase?
- Is the keyword in the site name, the name of the page, or the text of the page?
- Are they saying something like your keyword could be where to find black prom dresses and their title is where to find black prom dresses? That means that people are specifically targeting that keyword.
- How long has the site and page been in existence (older sites have better rankings)
- Are there other websites linking to the website? (you can use AHREF or Semrush to get some of these numbers)
- Are there other websites linking to the exact page with the keyword? (you can use AHREF or Semrush to get some of these numbers)
- Step 3 Tally the yes and number for all of the questions for each of the top sites
- Step 4 evaluate how competitive the tops sites are. The more yes and higher numbers you have for the above questions the more competitive your keywords are. If you just have 1 or 2 sites with high numbers that pretty safe, 3-7 is somewhat competitive, anything more than that is very competitive

In LongTailPro, they give you what they call the KC, the keyword competitiveness score. In Keywords Everywhere, they give you just the high, low, medium. For LongTailPro, you want to stay under 30 with that competitive score, and I have a video on the resource section for this for you guys.

It really depends on the tools, so make sure you look at the tool and see how they calculate their competitiveness.

EXERCISE

Analysis Exercise

In this exercise, I'm giving you a handy chart to keep track of your keywords as you work through the analysis. You can use this chart over and to keep track of your keywords. I'm also adding a date column. Keyword numbers change over time it's a good Idea to keep track of when you research a keyword. If it's been a few months research them again to update numbers.

After you've completed the analysis check them off the top 10-15 with the best numbers to move on to the next step

	Keyword	Search Volume	Competitive Score	Date
1				
2				
3				
4				
5				
6				
7				
8				
9				
10				

Note: these numbers change, so the numbers that you get for something today may change slightly within six months or three months. As people search during different times of the year or the competition gets stiffer the numbers will shift. You want to do some keyword research and checking for keywords at least every couple of months just to double check your words.

Connecting

Most people end their keyword at the analysis step, but over the years I've learned ending there leads people to have keywords that don't really fit their business, are difficult for them to work it, and ultimately don't get the results they want.

Once you've gone through the Analysis, and you've gotten a group of good keywords now is the time to validate that they'll work for you. In the next 2 steps of the R.A.C.E. method, we test the keywords we've found are going to work for you and your audience. This step is pretty simple, but I found it to be one of the most valuable in keyword research.

We validate the keywords by beginning to connect them to what you do and prep for future content.

Making the Connection

- **Give them a category,** most website's blogs have categories you use to group together the blog post and topics your cover on your site. For this first step, I want you to put the 10-15 keywords we ended analysis within 3-4 categories.

    If you have difficulty assigning a category to a keyword, it might not connect well with your business. Or
    if you have to many categories like ten categories for 15 keywords that means your keywords are too broad and unrelated, this will cause your content to be all over the place.

A Keywords	B Volume	C Competitive Score	D Categories
scriptures on finances	2900	33	finance education info
scriptures on freedom	1600	31	finance education info
financial freedom quotes	590	31	finance education info
budget for family of 4	320	34	budget help
household budget percentages	260	28	budget help
family meal planner on a budget	210	29	budget help
financial independence blog	480	25	financial freedom
financial freedom	8100	31	finance freedom
how to get out of debt fast	1600	35	finance freedom
validation of debt letter	2400	34	financial tools

Here's an example of assigning keywords a category
This is one of my mastermind members last year; her site is in the financial services niche. I reduced the list for this example, but the full list was about 40 keywords we put into five categories.

- Next step to connecting is **making sure you can create content for the keyword**. Sometimes we have a great keyword but when it's time to write you're stumped om if this is something you can talk about.

We complete our connecting step by brainstorming 50 blog post title for your keywords. Don't panic this is just brainstorming. In the next chapter, I'm going to jump into writing using these keywords and what kind of information people look for, but in this step I want you to start thinking of topics on your own. The idea is you want keywords that you know enough about to write something without being prompted. If you struggle with ideas for the keyword in this step, it's a good sign that those keywords don't fit your business well. 50 is a really safe number because usually after the first 10, you'll see around 10, 20, it gets a little bit more difficult. 50 is going to be a stretch and, if you can stretch it, that means it's really applicable to your business and really something you can work with.

> **HINT:** If you need a little help with this step. Use AnswerThePublic (one of the tools we discussed in chapter 2). Answer the Public can give you questions people are asking about your keyword. Review the questions they give and determine which would you be able to answer and write about. You can also questions tag

Engage

This is the last part of our R.A.C.E Method. Remember SEO is all about speaking your customers' language. But speaking it is not enough you also want to make sure they understand and get what you are saying. I don't want you to wait until you've written 10 blog post and/or built a whole site to make sure keywords will resonate with your audience, so in this last step, we start testing out your keywords to see how your potential customers respond to them.

The testing is pretty easy; you can begin using the keywords to engage with your audience in groups and social media and see if they respond with silence and crickets or a hardy "yesssss, girl, that's so me."

An example using the finance keywords above:

Keyword: Budget for a family of 4
Social Media Post: "Here are few tips I learned working a budget for a family of 4...." "Budgeting for a family of 4 has been one of the biggest challenges my clients have had in 2018."

Keyword: Scriptures for Freedom
"Today I read this scripture for freedom, and it inspired to stay on my journey to build my business. What scriptures for freedom have inspired you?"

> "What are your favorite scriptures for freedom."

You see the testing doesn't have to be too intensive just start using the keywords you've found in the conversations and post you are already sharing online; this will give you an idea of what your audience likes and maybe even give you more topics for chapter 6.

That's our race method, by the end of this you should have at least 5 main keywords to focus on throughout your site and a few lesser keywords that you can use in a specific post.

But important you now have the skill to evaluate keywords and keep going back to find more and more opportunities to rank.

I usually start a site with 5 focus words and revisit this method every few months when I want to expand my content into another area. For example, when I started my site focused on building a boutique and researched keywords in that area, over the years I have talked more about blogging, affiliates, and SEO for each area I revisit the RACE method to get keyword that fits best for that subjects.

Lastly, when I have a new blog post or podcast episode I do a bit on the A-analysis part of the RACE to see if there are words that fit in the post that I'll have better chances of ranking.

In the next chapter, we'll talk about where and how to use all of these keywords. So buckle your seatbelt and get ready for content.

The Ranking Checklist

1) **Initial site checks**
   - ✓ Confirm Google analytics access (Chapter 2)
   - ✓ Confirm Google search console (Chapter 2)
   - ✓ Get Current Metrics (Chapter 2)
   - ✓ Do initial site readiness checks (Chapter 4)
     - ✓ 404 errors
     - ✓ Address URL issues
     - ✓ Blank descriptions
     - ✓ Duplicate content
     - ✓ Broken links
     - ✓ Blank alt tags

2) **Complete keyword research (Chapter 5)**
   - ✓ Round Up- Create list of potential keywords
   - ✓ Analyze- Check volume and competition for keywords
   - ✓ Connect- Create a potential list of topics and categories
   - ✓ Engage- Test your words out in post and on social
   - ✓ Select 5-10 focus keywords

3) **Update Content on site**
   - ☐ Add keywords to pages on your site (Chapter 6)
   - ☐ Find Update images (Chapter 6)
   - ☐ Update page tags, descriptions, headings, images, etc. (Chapter 6)
   - ☐ Choose SEO friendly topics (Chapter 7)
   - ☐ Choose blog post types you like (Chapter 7)
   - ☐ Write 5-10 blog post (Chapter 7)

4) **Internal inks (Chapter 8)**
   - ☐ Identify pages without links
   - ☐ Identify pages to link to on your site
   - ☐ Create internal links

5) **External Linking (Chapter 8)**
   - ☐ Find link building opportunities
   - ☐ Fid group to collaborate with
   - ☐ Monitor incoming links

6) **Wrap up and ongoing (Chapter 9)**
   - ☐ Schedule future blog post
   - ☐ Pitch link building opportunities
   - ☐ Update target keywords
   - ☐ Complete Monthly Look back and plan ahead
   - ☐ Monthly 2-4 blog post with internal link
   - ☐ Monthly 5-10 backlinks

Chapter 6 Words Matter

People won't talk to you if you aren't speaking their language.

How content and keywords mix

Now that you've R.A.C.Ed It's time to talk a little bit about where to put those words on your site and the type of content you're going to create.

Content is any words, or text, or even images and videos that you put on your website. Most times we refer to the blogging part of content because words matter to Google, but I'll also talk a little bit about how you can make videos, and images work as good content of your site as well.

> **TIP:** Remember Google only reads words and text. It reads text in a form of code, and it's important that you actually put some text on your site. Even if you've got a video blog, VG, or a catalog with images, you still need to have text in and on your site so that Google can understand what those videos and images are.

Keywords are the hooks for your site, they are what people are going to google for, and what people are going to see in the little search engine blurb before the click in. They hook people into visiting your site, once they get hooked into your site, the content is what's actually going to sell about you and your product. You don't want to just go putting a bunch of keywords on your site without putting some content and context around them to really sell into what you do.

When I say sell, not just selling your products and getting a cash exchange; but selling includes signing up for your email list, getting to follow your blog, recommending you to others, etc. Everything that will have them continuing to engage with your site and your business is what your content is going to do for you.

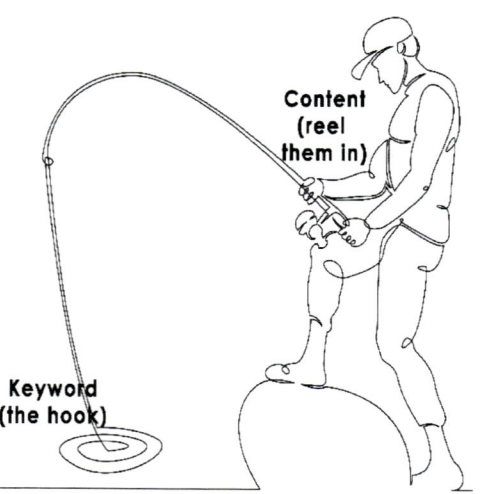

What makes good SEO content?

Content isn't just what's on your blog, every page on your site is seen as content to Google. Google reads every page (with the exception of a few that are blocked but don't worry about those right now). Each page is indexed and has the ability to be ranked in search results. I've seen really good ranks where the same site will take up multiple spots on page 1 for a search term.

You'll want to use keywords throughout the pages, tags, and titles of your site. You want to incorporate them into your normal sentences and paragraphs, consider them part of the new language you speak to your customers. Be careful to avoid using random strings of keyword that don't read like real sentences. This is called **keyword stuffing.**

> **Good Keyword text examples:**
> This is the About Page text on my retail site, I've underlined all of the places where keywords are used.
>
> Need a new Sorority Gift Idea?
>
> What <u>sorority member</u> doesn't love <u>sorority gear and apparel</u> with their <u>Sorority Greek Letters</u> on it?
>
> Stationary makes the best <u>Sorority Gift Idea</u> and Color Me Finer is a **<u>premier stationary company</u>** that provides greeting cards, note cards, thank you cards, and **custom stationery for <u>black sororities and organizations.</u>**
>
> You can give as a gift or include a card with the <u>black Greek apparel</u> you are gifting.
>
> Our goal is to help enhance your <u>organization's presence</u> with professional and unique designs that <u>represent your sorority or fraternity</u>."
>
> **Bad Keyword Text Example:**
>
> "We can help your business with copywriting, graphics, brochures, cards, templates, books, printing, print screening and all your needs in the North New Jersey Passaic County, Essex County, Bergen County, Morris County, Sussex County areas.
>
> Groups helped: Mom's clubs, sports teams, PAL, PBA, Greek organizations, local businesses (including contractors, landscapers, plumbers, roofers) and school districts. "

Do you see the difference in how the 2 are worded one puts different keywords throughout the paragraphs so I can be easily read, the other is just a string of keywords? Now that we have an idea of how to write with keywords, let's look at that information and keywords should go on each page of your site

How to SEO the pages of your site

About Page

On your about to page, you want to talk about how you help you help people and sprinkle in a few keywords. This is where you want to go into who you work with, how you benefit them, and maybe intertwine a little bit of story of how you came to this conclusion that you can do this. *Your about page is not about you, it's about them.*

Contact page

Your contact page doesn't have to have a lot of content, but it is a good place to sneak in your keywords and searchable statement. Phrases like

- "If you're looking for ..." name some of your services, or name some of the types of information,
    - Example: If you're looking for downloads, or freebies, or resources on starting an online boutique, click here. If you're looking for services and SEO click here.
- If you'd like to contact us to talk about services or products for SEO, or online retail click here, or fill out this form."

On your contact, you should also put an address or city and state you operate in if you have a physical lotion. This will help with local and location-based searched even if you're always online, you still want to put some information about your location because this will help you to show up in those searches better

Homepage

When I do my website reviews I see a lot of homepages that really don't tell you anything about what you're going to get from this site which makes them bad for user experience and bad for SEO.

Your Homepage should immediately answer 2 questions 1) who you serve and 2) how you serve them. You don't need a lot of words on the page even a few keywords thrown into a tag live like "Affordable fashion options for busy moms" or "Teach retail entrepreneurs how to get found in search"
Both of these lines are easy for users to read and easy for Google to pick up. You can also add text about other things like your products, the ways you help people, why people should work with you. But at the least, you want your homepage to say who you serve and how you serve them.

Service pages

On your services page, you can expand on what on your homepage adding in additional information and keywords to hook the visitor. I write my services out a little bit more in depth like a mini sales page. I use the text on this page to introduce services, answer major questions, and talk about my target customer a.k.a use LOTS of keywords.

If you head over to onlineboutiquesource.com/SEO, you'll see an example of my service page. I didn't want to just say, "Hey, we do SEO services." But I wanted to take some time to educate people on the importance of SEO, on what SEO means, and how my services can help them with SEO. That's a lot of extra words right?

Also don't be afraid to have separate services pages for different services you have. If you have multiple services or services that break down into more specific services have one main service page and additional pages to go into more detail about the specific offer.

Resource pages

Resource pages are pages that where you list resources where people can find additional information and help. Everyone may not have a resource page but if you do treat it as SEO content, a good way to do this for each resource give a sentence or 2 about why this page is relevant to your target audience and how the same.

On a resource page you can list different software people can use, you can list different services that are out there. An example is my previous Sickle Cell Foundation client, on their site we had a resource page that listed other sickle sites, medical information, local programs etc.

FAQ page

FAQ (Frequently Asked Questions) page is a really good place to answer all of the questions you get about your niche, products, business policies etc. FAQ pages are my absolute favorite for extra SEO because they have to be long drawn out answers but they are still super valuable to your audience. You can start with a small FAQ page, maybe answer 5 or 6 questions and grow as you get more questions and keyword ideas.

HINT: Don't only talk about your business in your FAQs but also answer a few industry-related questions that people have.

Policies and Disclaimers

Your policies could be your shipping policy, your return policy, your privacy policy, all of those are pages are content on your site. Similar to your FAQ you don't just want to talk about the things that are relevant to your business, but also include general policy terms that people search for expedited shipping, refund, guarantees, industry-specific credentials (like ABC certified). You can Even throw in some myth busters, "Some businesses may take up to four weeks or may take delayed shipping. We provide rush shipping and service options that are standard or not standard in the industry." My previous bridal shop client The Last Minute Bride we did this with her site where he does fast shipping, which is something that last minute brides would be looking for.

On policy pages, you again want to talk about the type of people that you help, who you help, and how you help them. Those are really the most important things that you're going to say a lot over and over, and over again. You can add more descriptive details about your business in these little different bits of content in different places, example "The information that you find here about SEO and online retail will definitely help you, but results differ per site and industry." There you gave a disclaimer, but you also threw in the kind of information that you're giving them.

These are just some of the major pages that could be on your site but every page is considered content and where possible you want to incorporate your SEO keywords.

But, Am I just repeating yourself?

As you're reading through all of these pages, I know you're concerned that you may be repeating yourself, covering the same information, and using some of the same keywords over and over; don't worry, that's normal, and it's actually good for your reader.

"tell 'em what you're going to say, say it, and then tell 'em what you said."

This quote is true for teaching and building a good SEO site. Saying the same thing multiple times and in multiple ways on your site is a good way to enforce your message and for Google to understand what your site is about.

So don't worry about repeating yourself; just make sure you mix the words up, so it's not duplicate content.

Product Description Formula

In this section, we'll discuss product descriptions. I separated this from the other pages because like blogs, product descriptions will represent a big chunk of the content on most sites, especially retailers. My number 1 rule for product descriptions is to WRITE YOUR OWN!!!! Too often I see online retailers using the descriptions provided by their wholesalers or seen on other sites. This is considered duplicate content and could hurt your site.

The product description is such an important part of E-commerce sites and their SEO, I created a whole formula to make sure you get this part right.

The **product descriptions formula** is of a combination of using content, image, and SEO to drive people to want to purchase your products.

The product description is the most important part of the online retail website, besides the buy button, of course. It is what makes someone want to own your product – the product – and close the sale.

The idea of your product description page is to help them envision themselves with your product and entice them to buy. Weak product description pages are one of the top reasons why people visit sites and don't purchase anything. Another huge reason to love on your descriptions is that they are great for SEO.

In this document, I'll review each section of the product description page and how you can set up and make sure yours rock!

Sections of Your Product description:

- **The Title**
  The title is a unique description of the item. Use no more than 5–7 words. If possible, include 1–2 keywords that are relevant to the product. Make sure each title on your site is unique.

  Common mistakes: avoid using the wholesalers' title, avoid using names and other words that don't describe the items, i.e., Bella's dress.

- **Main Image**
  The main image should clearly show the item and be consistent with other product images. We'll talk about this later in tags, but make sure the title and alt tag tell you what's in the pictures.

- **Additional images**
  The more you can help someone experience your product, the better your conversions will be. Most sites allow you to add 3–4 different images to the listing. USE THEM ALL!!! Add additional views of the product, the product in use, the product shown with other products in a lookbook fashion and give a descriptive title and alt tag to each photo.

- **Short description**
  This is where you want to paint a picture of life with your products. The description should be about 4–5 lines on the screen – not too long or short. Start with a catchy phrase; Who the item is great for, what the item is great for, 1–2 benefits of owning the item, any unique features that make it stand out from similar items, and sprinkle in SEO keywords where possible.

  Example: Elegant Notecards for the ladies of Zeta Phi Beta Sorority, Inc. This note card has the popular chevron print in royal blue and white and shows off your sorority pride with the sorority's new seal.

- **Long Description**
  This is where you get all of the technical stuff. Sizes, colors, material, ingredients, any care instructions, etc. This can be a great area for SEO if you are specific with these details and understand what's important to your audience. People often search for items based on ingredients and feature that are important to them (e.g., Hair oil with Coconut Oil or Faux leather), and they also may search without information, e.g., Paraben.

A good way to separate the short and long description is, the short description makes them want to buy, while the long description answers the questions they have to close the sale. If your site only has one description box, feel free to combine the two.

- Reviews
  When possible, get 3–4 reviews per item. You can't control what's in a review, but a review is additional text on your pages and usually mentions some of the keywords that are important to your customers. So, encourage reviews often, and encourage people to leave them on your site where it will help you the most, not just on social media.
- Tags
  Tags are an old SEO holdover. Many search engines don't look at them anymore, but you should still use them for those that do, and they give a little more information to the customer on sites that display them. Put 5–7 phrases that your product fits into. Don't go overboard. These aren't like IG hashtags.

EXERCISE

Create your own product description

Take one of your favorite products and use the diagram below to start mapping out what your product description will look like. For each section, put the text you will use on your site, and for the images, write the title and alt tag you will use. To make it even more fun, count how many keywords you can fit in each section (note: it's ok to repeat the same keyword in different sections just a few times).

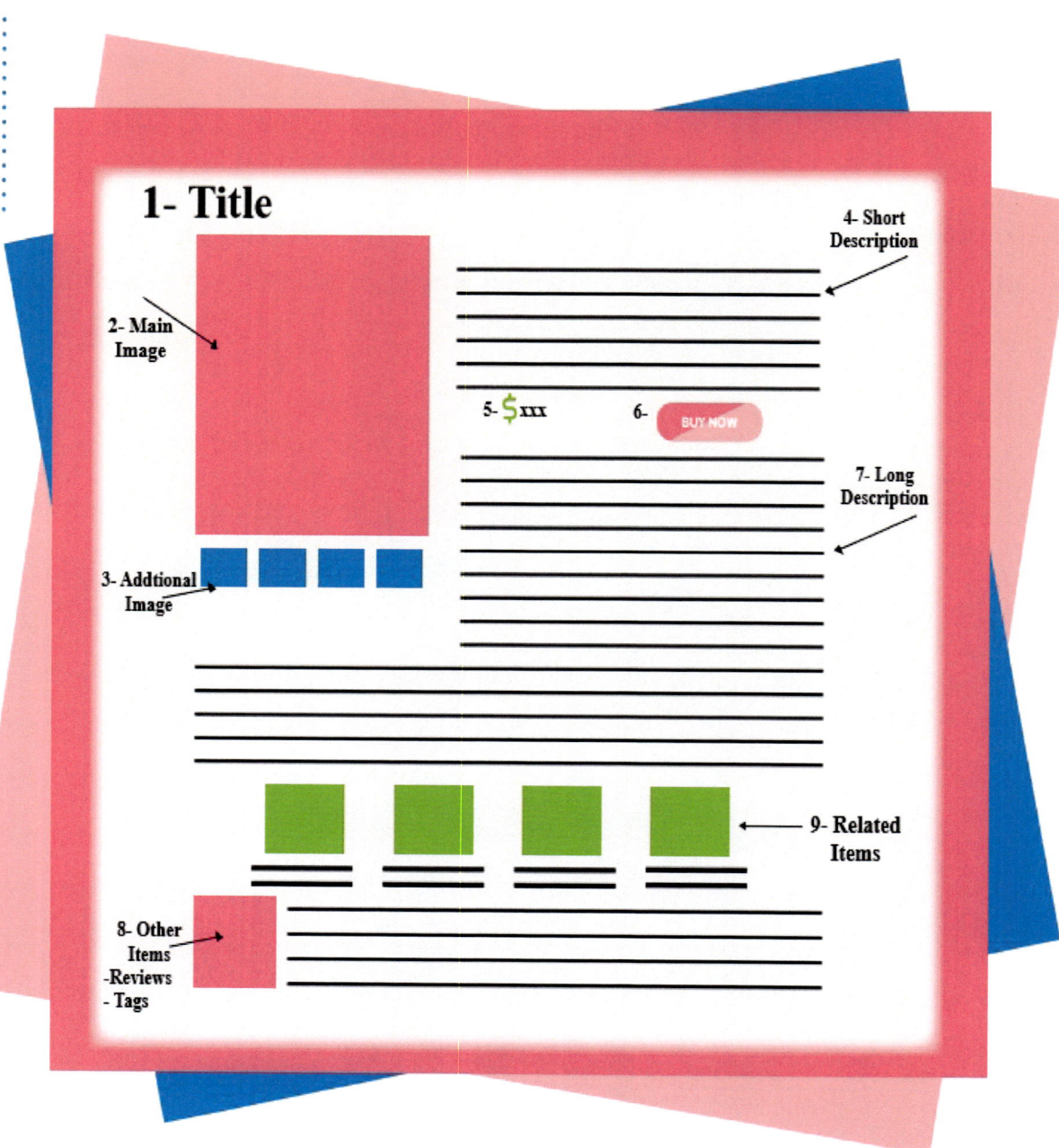

What really makes up your site, the code and tags

Most of today's website builder platforms are **content management systems (CMS)** that let you build full websites without touching codes. The CMS will build the code for you based on the selections you make and the fields you populate when you create your pages and blog post. I'm not going to teach coding in this book; I'm going to focus of the definition and use of some of the options, so that you are able to see what these different functions are in writing your posts.

This is where a lot of the SEO tools like Yoast SEO plugin, or the SEO fields in Shopify and Squarespace come in.

Websites are made up of HTML codes (hypertext mark-up language). Browsers read HTML, and they know where to put the words, images, buttons on your site.

Don't Panic, but this is what your pretty website looks like to Google:

Again, you don't need to know how to write or even read this for good SEO. You'll only need to know how to use the buttons and dropdowns that make this happen.

Most Website Builders have a toolbar where you create pages and posts that looks something like this:

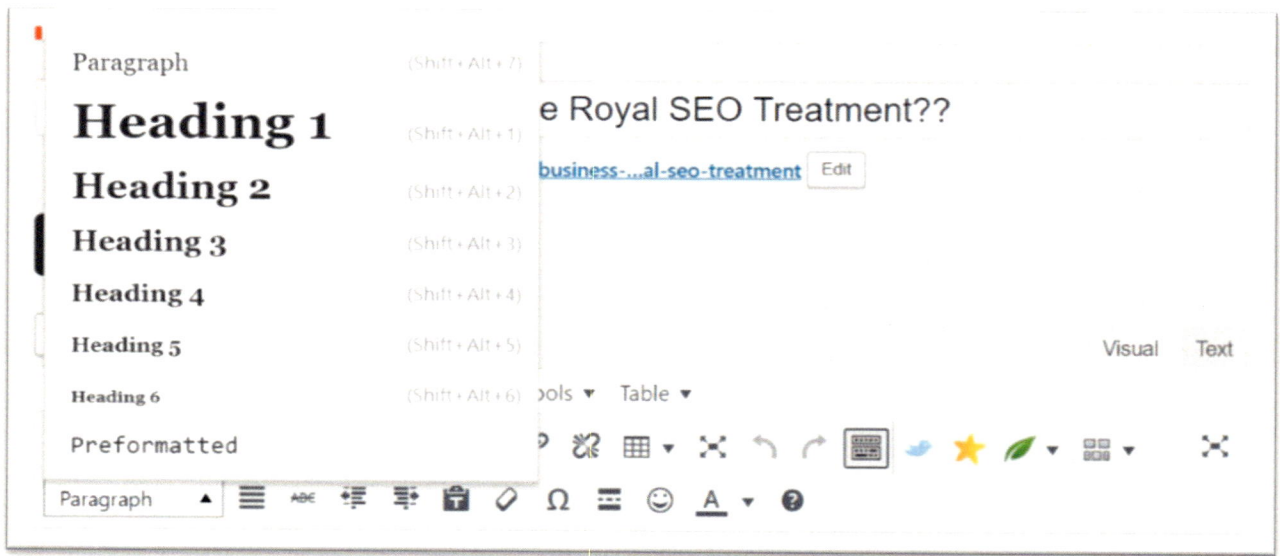

Here's what dropdowns and HTML fields mean and how you should use them (visit the resource site for a video overview of HTML).

Heading 1 (also knowns as H1 or header1)

Header1 tells browsers what the most important text on your page is – the title. Even though there are options to create a header1 tag, you only want one header1 per page, and that would be your page title. I don't recommend using the header1 at all when you're creating your blog posts and pages.

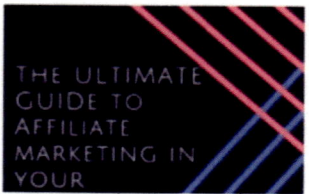

Headings 2, 3, 4, 5, 6

It's a good idea to break up your longer pages into chunks of information using subtitles. Just like an outline, you can show the levels of information by using these Heading tags. Tags 1, 2, 3 tell Google how important these words are on the site. Heading 1 is the most important, 2 is the next important, 3 is pretty important, and then there's 4, 5, and 6 that show subscript information like footnotes. Instead of just reading top to bottom, using heading tags, Google can tell what's most important and what's not so. It's good to use keywords in the Heading tags as much as possible, but don't use the same keywords over and over, as you want to sprinkle your keywords into the sections Google will see first.

Here's an example of post outline:

```
Header 1: Title
    Header 2 – Main Subtitle
        Header 3 – Subtitle under Main title
        Header 3 – Subtitle under Main Title
            Header 5 – footnote
    Header 2 – Another Main Subtitle
        Header 3 – Subtitle under Main title
    Header 4 – smaller subtitle
    Header 5 – Footnote
    Header 3 – Subtitle under Main Title
```

***As you can see, you don't have to use each Heading type on your page.

Paragraph tag (P)

The paragraph tag is for any text that is not part of the other tags. This is a majority of the text on your page – the real meat of your content are in paragraphs. You normally don't have to assign a paragraph tag as anything that is not in another tag is automatically made a paragraph.

TIP: The hierarchy of content is very important to search engines, but don't try to make everything important by overusing headings. You want to be very specific about what's important and what's not as important. Google is going to read everything.

Bold tag

You'll see this on your website builder as a **B**, and it'll make the text thicker, so it stands out on the page. A lot of times, I see people use the bold tag for their subtitles. Don't do that. Use the header tags for your subtitles, and only use bold when you want to make specific words or sentences bold. Search Engines will see these words as important but not as important as the heading. This also helps users know when they should pay attention.

Underlining

You can underline text on your website to draw attention, but I don't recommend doing this. Over the years, readers have been training that underlined words link to another page or site. We've gotten so accustomed to this that when you see an underline, and it doesn't move, it's just weird. For usability purposes, only use underline if it's linking out to another page, or another site, something somebody can click on.

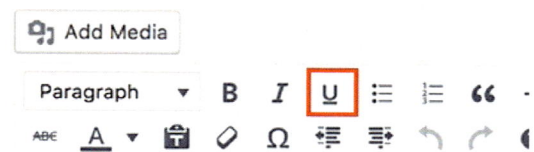

Bullets

We've all seen bullets in Word or in a presentation, but did you know there are codes behind them too? There are two types of bullets in HTML – UL Unordered list and OL ordered list. UL will give you the round bullets you're used to, and OL will give you a numbered list. Lucky for us, website builders have little bullet and numbered list buttons. This lets search engines know that the texts on these lists go together, and it also looks a lot nicer than using dashes or asterisks to fake a list.

Now that we've covered most of the tags and codes you see on a screen, here's a diagram of what this all looks like on an actual web page.

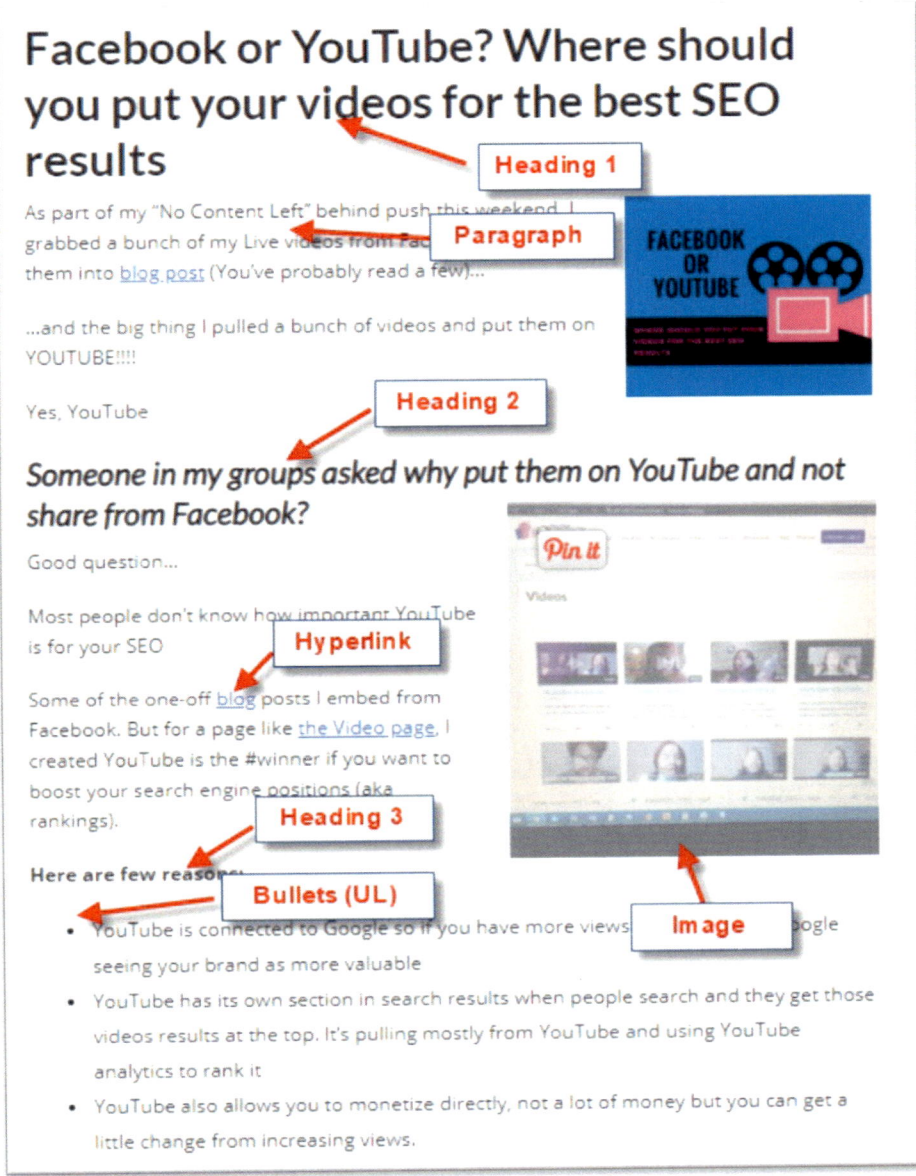

But we're not done with tags and codes yet. There are a number of fields that do not show up on the screen and are only read by search engines and browsers. These fields are important too because they give search engines more information about what's on the page and where they should index it.

Alt tag

We've talked about this a little bit before. Alt tags are the tags that go with your images. Alt tag is the text that is shown if for some reason, someone is using an assisted disability device, or the picture doesn't come up, but it also tells Google what your picture is about. Most systems, when you upload the image, you have the option to set a title and alt tag. I want you to use both of them. Do not leave your title as IMG.12345.jpg, and don't leave your alt tag empty.

Google can't see pictures. You have to give it a nudge to say, "This is what this picture is." The alt tag is really, really important for disability purposes, but also for Google to know what's in the picture.

> **TIP:** When I'm adding pictures of myself, or of a person or something like that, instead of saying, "Picture of Akilah," I would say, "Picture of SEO strategist," or, "A picture of top SEO strategist in New Jersey." I like to put it by the title or something that I want to be known for because when people are searching for an SEO strategist in New Jersey, I want to pop up as my picture, my face. No one is going to search for Akilah. I'm okay with that; I'd rather show up for what I do.

Meta tags

You can think of your meta tags like categories. What category would this be in? Like if I'm talking about SEO, I might do an 'SEO tips,' 'blogging tips.' I might do just three or four different things to put in as my meta tags. Meta tags aren't as important to Google anymore. People were abusing them, so Google doesn't reference them that much, but I still like to give 3-4 meta tags for each post for other search engines and to help users find the post on my site. Google doesn't look at them as much anymore, but Yahoo and Bing are back and forth on it, but I like to have at least something populated because it helps people to see that these things go together.

Categories

Speaking of categories, most blogging systems, I know of WordPress, allows you to put posts in categories. If you go back to when we were doing our keyword list in the last chapter, you'll remember we set categories. Use those categories on your blog. It's important for SEO purposes, but also, it assists people looking for information on your site. Many related-post plugins also use categories to organize your content. It's a good idea to have 4–5 good ones. Don't have too many, as it gets too confusing. If you don't have the ability to put posts in categories, I would consider getting a new website platform. Categories really help usability, and it helps with your SEO too.

Page Description

Page descriptions are the little bit of text that you will see when a site comes up in the search results. The text, by default, is the first few lines of text on your page, but most website builders and the Yoast Plugin let you override the default with a blurb that you can write. The blurb should give searches an idea of what the page is about. This blurb is what helps people decide if they should click onto your site or not. A good blurb can help to drastically increase your click-through rates (CTR we discussed earlier).

Two things to make sure you have in your page description:

A) it's something that people are going to understand what it is about

B) it's something that contains a few of your keywords. You want to keep that less than 160 characters.

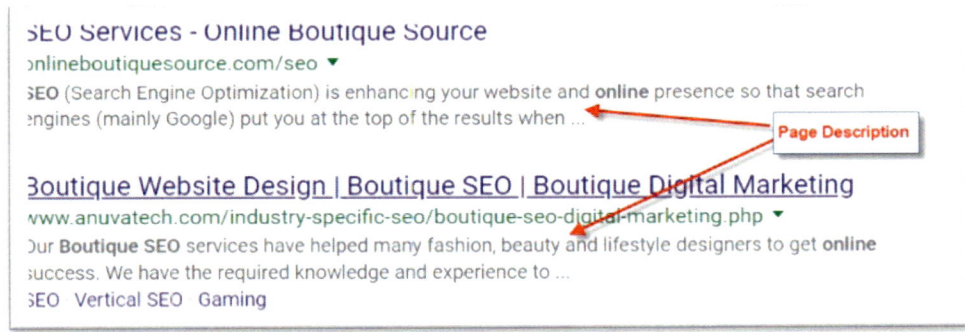

Now that you understand more about the tags and codes you should be using on your site, we want to do a quick audit of your top pages to make sure they contain all of the elements we discussed in this section.

My SEO Workbook

> **EXERCISE**
>
> Let's check out your site!!!
>
> In this exercise, use the checklist below to audit your top 10 pages. If a page does have one of the elements on the list, edit the page to ensure you have the correct tags.
>
> Find your top pages by looking in Google Search Console and Google Analytics. Top pages are those already ranking for any keywords, pages getting the most traffic, service pages, blog posts that get the most engagement when shared.
>
> You can continue auditing other pages after this exercise, but the idea is to focus on the ones that will get you the best results first.

Page Name	Header 1	Headers 2-6	Bullets	Paragraph	Category (post only)	Image Title/Alt Tag	Meta Tags	Page description

The Ranking Checklist

1) **Initial site checks**
   - ✓ Confirm Google analytics access (Chapter 2)
   - ✓ Confirm Google search console (Chapter 2)
   - ✓ Get Current Metrics (Chapter 2)
   - ✓ Do initial site readiness checks (Chapter 4)
     - ✓ 404 errors
     - ✓ Address URL issues
     - ✓ Blank descriptions
     - ✓ Duplicate content
     - ✓ Broken links
     - ✓ Blank alt tags

2) **Complete keyword research (Chapter 5)**
   - ✓ Round Up- Create list of potential keywords
   - ✓ Analyze- Check volume and competition for keywords
   - ✓ Connect- Create a potential list of topics and categories
   - ✓ Engage- Test your words out in post and on social
   - ✓ Select 5-10 focus keywords

3) **Update Content on site**
   - ✓ Add keywords to pages on your site (Chapter 6)
   - ✓ Find Update images (Chapter 6)
   - ✓ Update page tags, descriptions, headings, images, etc. (Chapter 6)
   - ☐ Choose SEO friendly topics (Chapter 7)
   - ☐ Choose blog post types you like (Chapter 7)
   - ☐ Write 5-10 blog post (Chapter 7)

4) **Internal inks (Chapter 8)**
   - ☐ Identify pages without links
   - ☐ Identify pages to link to on your site
   - ☐ Create internal links

5) **External Linking (Chapter 8)**
   - ☐ Find link building opportunities
   - ☐ Fid group to collaborate with
   - ☐ Monitor incoming links

6) **Wrap up and ongoing (Chapter 9)**
   - ☐ Schedule future blog post
   - ☐ Pitch link building opportunities
   - ☐ Update target keywords
   - ☐ Complete Monthly Look back and plan ahead
   - ☐ Monthly 2-4 blog post with internal link
   - ☐ Monthly 5-10 backlinks

Chapter 7 Blogs Glorious Blogs

Your site has to say for google to know you do it.

We've got the rest of the site in order, now let's talk about a Major Part of your content.

THE BLOG!!!
A blog is a content you regularly share on your site in the form of articles and post. The blog's role is to inform, educate, and entertain your readers on topics around your industry and business.

WARNING: This isn't a blogging book! I'm going to focus on blogging for SEO, how the blog can help SEO, and how to use a blog easily and effectively for your business. There are some things you NEED to do as a blogger that can differ from what we do for SEO.
Before you tell me what the "blog guru" said, remember we want to be #1 in search, not America's Next top blogger :D

You don't HAVE to blog to get SEO (we'll talk about that at the end of the chapter), but blogging, or at least, publishing a few blog posts, sometimes will help you get better results much faster.

Just in case I need to convince you that you really should not skip blogging, here are 3 Reasons you should blog for your business;

1. It gives you an opportunity to use more keywords and discuss different topics and subtopics on your site
2. It shows off your knowledge and expertise in your niche and often shows visitors how you can help them
3. It creates shareable content that can be shared on social media, referenced in other articles and sites, and used to answer questions.

BONUS: It helps establish an authority. People listen to the person who talks about or writes about a topic the most, and the more you blog, you are building your authoritative space.

OK, now that I've got you ready to blog, for the rest of this chapter, we'll focus on these.

Writing a good post is a little more than putting your thoughts on paper. In this book, we'll break down blogging into three major steps, T.T.P. (Topic, Type, Post It). Using the TTP steps, you'll get what to write about, the format to write it in, and how to post it on your site. First, we're going to choose topics about your keywords that relate to your brand. Second, we're going to write the blog post using one of the many blog post types, and last, we'll talk on publishing the post on your site.

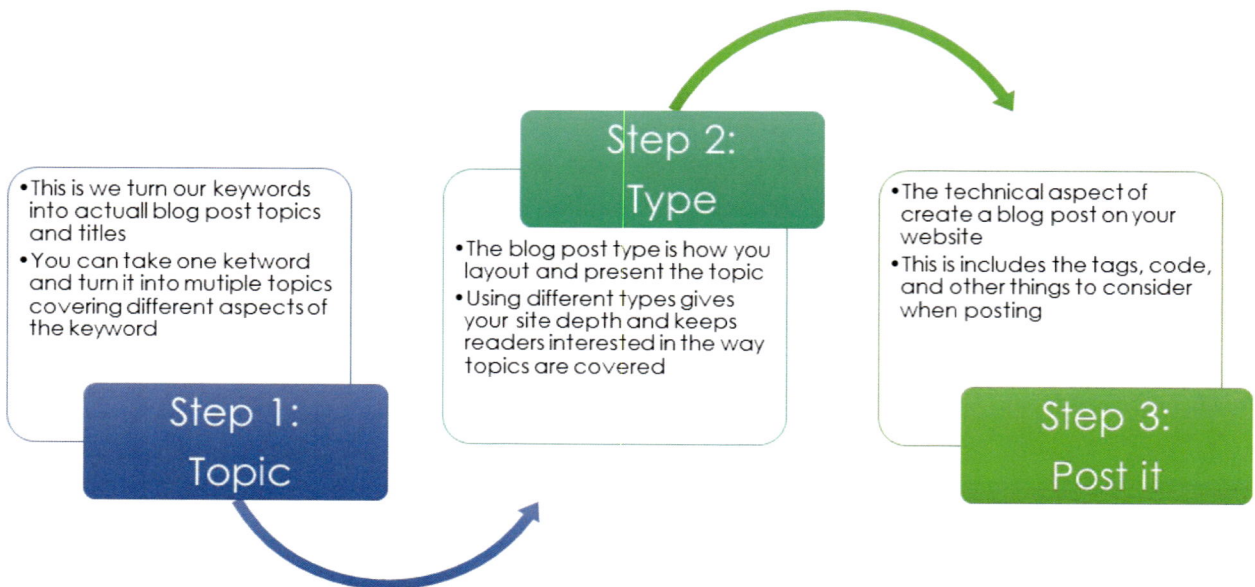

Step 1: Choosing topics

Here, we pick up where we left off with our keyword research. There are several ways to choose what you want to write about. I recommend rotating through these strategies and selecting a few for each one.

The Basics

The basics (aka The Eggs, Milk and Butter) are the beginner topics about your niche or industry. What are the first things people need to know to get started, the building blocks? The basic would be topics like:
- "What supplies do I need?"
- "What's the best way to get started?"
- "A checklist of the main steps."
- "A business plan to get started."

I like to refer to these as the eggs, milk, and butter, because they are the key ingredients that someone needs to begin to make the final result. Chapter 1 of this book would be the Eggs, Milk, and Butter of SEO.

The Assumptions

The next topic strategy is to break down the assumptions. These are the posts about things everyone knows or should know, but you'd be surprised at how many do not. A lot of times, because we work in the industry, we understand the jargons and concepts like they are second nature, but we had to learn them from somewhere, and with these topics, your reader can learn from you.

I often give the example of when I went to the Burger King drive-through and they assumed that I knew what Pepsi products were, when in reality, I don't drink soda much, so I had to ask the cashier to list the sodas that are considered Pepsi products.

A lot of people don't know what your niche industry is about and don't know all of the nuances until you tell them that information. The assumptions are a step-up from the basics. If the basics are the eggs, milk, and butter of a recipe, the assumptions are where you start describing how you mix them up.

Example: in the clothing industry, a lot of people may know what a peplum top is, but your average shopper may just see it as a cute shirt with the ruffle skirt thing on the bottom. You can do whole posts on breaking down some of those things that most people would assume. So a lot of times, assumptions around what are the different jargons.

The Frequent Questions

FAQs can be more than one page, where you break out questions and write a whole post about them. Think to yourself, what are the first questions or even the last questions that you've received about your niche or your industry? When you go into Facebook groups (I love Facebook groups for this), what are the key questions that people are asking? These questions could be and should be your next blog content. I always say, *"if one person is brave enough to ask a question out loud, there are probably 1000s of people with the same question in their head."*

Questions could be like, "Where can I find this?" "How does this compare to that?" There are a lot of different questions that people ask about a topic, and you can answer them. I started my site with a Q&A form on my website. When people asked questions, I answered by creating a blog post about it and sending the link.

Other good places to look for questions are:

- Answerthepublic.com
- Quora.com

- Questions you get in your comments/email/inbox/or working with clients.

Your Thoughts or Opinion Topics

There'll be different things in your industry that you have a strong opinion on, or you want to share about or teach in your own way, and this topic strategy is just for that. Part of being a thought leader or authority in your space is to share what you think, along with all of the other valuable content you give. Add in a few purely opinion or maybe even rant on your post. One of my mentors, Stu McLaren, often says, "there is no money in the middle." This is a good way to use your blog to share your voice and pick a side.

The Breakout

This is another version of how to break down some of the key aspects of your niche and products. This is where I take a main subject, and I break it down into subtopics and sub-sub-topics. Similar to a mind map, but in this case, every bubble is something you can write about.

Here's an example: If you're a virtual assistant, what are some of the big topics about being a virtual assistant? Maybe it's about time saving, money saving, or organization:

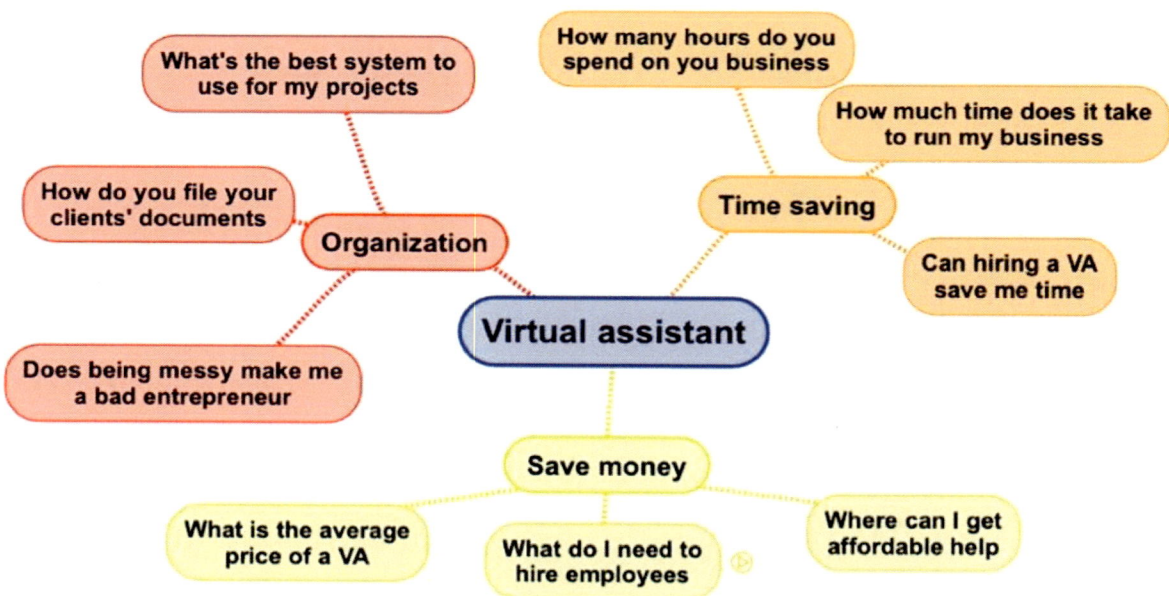

Doing a mind map and really drilling down into topics can give you dozens of other topics to choose from.

> **TIP:** You can use these groups of blog posts to help create epic blog posts and blog post series by linking grouped together blog posts. Take the main topic, like virtual assistance, write up an overview post mentioning the top three things that I've talked about, and then have smaller posts that link back to the main post and each other. We'll talk about linking in the next chapter, but know that this is great for SEO and readability.

Trending vs. Evergreen Topics

While we're on the topic of topics (you see what I did there, LOL), it's important to consider the longevity and immediate impact of your topic. Some topics will have a really quick impact because it is a hot topic of the day, and some will take a little longer to catch on but will last a long time. This is evergreen versus your trending topics.

Evergreen topics are like trees that will last through the test of time and gain more traction as they grow, and most business and product blogs are filled with evergreen content. Things that are a lot of your basics and assumptions, those will be evergreen posts that will ring true for a long-extended period of time. We use evergreen posts to be the anchor of our site and provide the content, answer those questions. Those are things that get searched a lot.

Trending topics are topics that are happening at a specific moment and are getting a lot of attention from their audience right now. Things like awards shows, the presidential election, or the Royals getting married. Trending are fast-moving, everyone is watching, but they quickly go away. Gossip blogs, political blogs, even some product sites (especially fashion) have more trending posts.

It's a good Idea to mix up trending and evergreen topics on your site. It's like building a fire – trending topics light the match and get quick traffic to your site, while evergreen is the wood and coals that keep things going at a slow burn.

My SEO Workbook

> **EXERCISE**
> In this exercise, I want you to come up with five topics from each of the different types. You can mix and match these on your actual blog, but each of these topics that you create now will help you with your writing later.
> Also, circle if the topic is trending or evergreen, and try to identify at least three trending topics for your list.

Basic Topics
- _____ T/E
- _____ T/E
- _____ T/E
- _____ T/E
- _____ T/E

Assumption Topics
- _____ T/E
- _____ T/E
- _____ T/E
- _____ T/E
- _____ T/E

Frequent Questions Topics
- _____ T/E
- _____ T/E
- _____ T/E
- _____ T/E
- _____ T/E

Opinion Topics
- _____ T/E
- _____ T/E
- _____ T/E
- _____ T/E
- _____ T/E

My SEO Workbook

EXERCISE

In this exercise, I want you to create your own breakout diagram. Choosing either one of your keywords from Chapter 5 or main topics for your niche, I want to break out at least three levels of topics that you can turn into blog posts.

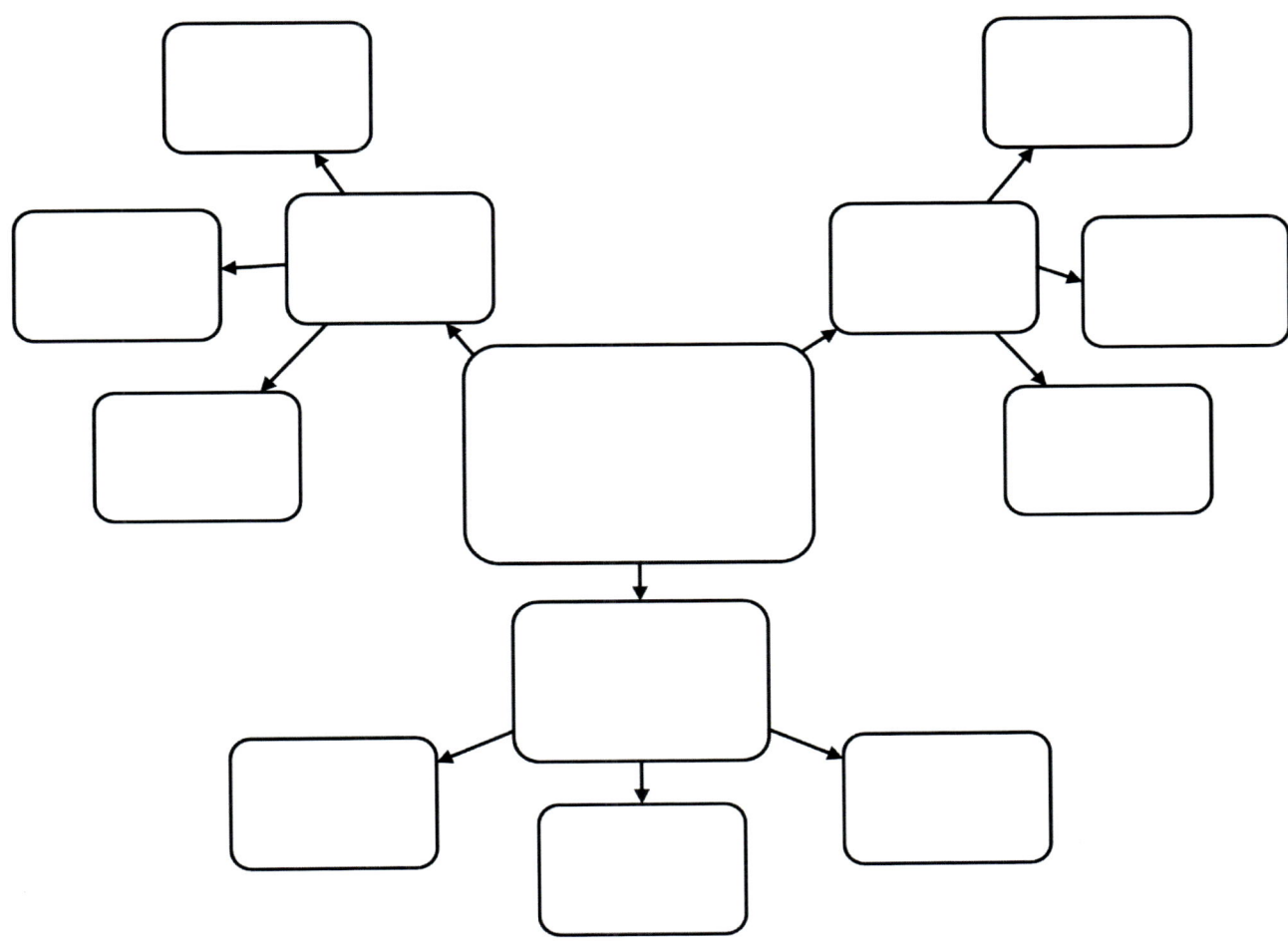

Step 2: Selecting Type

Next part of creating a blog is choosing the type or style you want to lay out your post in. The type helps determine how you will organize the post and sometimes the type of information you put in it.

Using different types will help keep people interested in your site and keep them coming back for more. You want to do different types of blog posts to add depth to your blog.

For example, if you want to do a how-to post, it would give step-by-step instructions on how to create something, while a list post would be like finished products.

Examples,

If I were writing about hardwood floors:

- How to: How to select the perfect hardwood for your home
- List Post: 5 Hardwood Patterns to choose for your home

There are many blog post types to choose from, and the list continues to grow as people come up with new ways to talk about stuff. In this book, we are going to focus on the top 11 that you see on most sites, and that will give your site plenty of varieties without overwhelming you. For each type, I'll also show you an example to give you an idea of what it will look like on a site, but some of the screenshots may be a little hard to read in print. To see the full post, I'll keep an updated list of links on the resource site:
http://onlineboutiquesource.com/seobookresources

List Post

A List post is where you list out a number of items related to the topic. You can create a list of books to read, things you learned from a recent event, lessons learned, etc. These are what we consider as list posts. Usually, list uses a 3, 5, 7 or a higher number like 2, 50, or 101.

When I create a short list of under 25, I'll usually write a little about each item listed, like I did here in this book. If it's a large list, 50 or more, I'll just put the name of the item and a few words.

Here's an example of a good list post:

5 Legal Notices you need on your Website today

HOME > 5 Legal Notices you need on your Website today

 ## 5 Legal Notices you need on your Website today

Is your website meeting legal guidelines? Do you know what legal notices you should have on your website, to ensure you and your site are protected? Many website owners skip adding legal notices to their site because they aren't sure that is needed and/or what it should say, today our Guest Blogger and Attorney Merissa V. Grayson from The Law Office of Merissa V. Grayson, is sharing with us the 5 Legal notices you should have on any website.

In today's society, there have been so many major technological advances over the last decade. We have gone from the pen and paper world, to the computer world, from classified newspapers and the yellow pages in the phone book, to the internet.

It's pretty much undisputed that an online presence is essential to success of any business or brand. Surprisingly, many people don't even consider the fact that an online presence comes with risks, rules, and consequences. If you're missing certain legal notices on your site, you may be at a higher risk of liability. You are probably breaking the laws of the online world yourself and don't even know it! But you're not alone, most people are… what is required of your website is not exactly clear-cut. Some websites require legal notices, some don't. The legal requirements that apply to your specific situation depend on the purpose of your website and how it functions. Many basic websites can get by with just a disclaimer and/or privacy policy; others may need more.

I know I know…it's a bit confusing. But, here are some of the standard notices all website owners should consider:

Disclaimer - A disclaimer is a statement about how people can use and access the information on your site. The purpose is to limit your liability for site visitors' use of the information or services provided by your site. Disclaimers are often used by those who have a lot of information and resources on their site such as blogs, articles, external links, etc. Common disclaimers include:

- **Site content**: If your site is informational (such as a blog), a disclaimer can inform users that the information on your site is for informational purposes only and should not be construed as professional advice.
- **User posted content**: If your site contains a forum or other means for visitors to submit comments or other content, a disclaimer can warn site visitors that the forum/contents are not monitored and may contain content that is not endorsed by you.
- **External Link**: If you and/or site users link to any outside websites or resources, a disclaimer can be used to clarify that you are not responsible for the site's accuracy, not endorsing the site and that the information in it is not your own.

Privacy Policy - Your site should have a privacy policy if you collect any type of information from site visitors such as email, phone numbers, addresses, names, gender, race, occupation, etc. The privacy policy tells site visitors about how the information is collected, how you will use the information collected, who that information is shared with, stored, and managed.

Terms and Conditions - Most websites should contain terms and conditions. Terms and conditions let site visitors know your site rules. This is how you let users know how they can and cannot use your website such as:

- How to credit content and/or pictures if they use it (i.e. crediting images, links back to the site, etc.)
- Whether site membership is required to post comments or other content
- Who can use your site: Age restrictions that (i.e. underage 15 requires adult permission), Geographical restrictions (i.e. If you are only licensed to conduct business in specific states/countries, etc.)
- Rights to use or remove-Situations that may result in users comments/comments being deleted (i.e. "spamming is not tolerated and will result in removal of your comments).
- Right to re-use or reproduce- lets users acknowledge that any content they submit to your site doesn't infringe on intellectual property laws and that they give you permission to re-use or reproduce it.

Intellectual Property Notice

How-To Post.

How-to posts are pretty common; these are posts where you give detailed instructions on how to accomplish an end result. This could be how to send an email to your customers or how to build a house. I try to keep my how-to posts very specific; something people can accomplish in a few hours or days. I wouldn't really do 'how to build a house,' but I would do 'how to sheetrock a room,' 'how to lay down flooring,' or 'how to install a sink.' Keep it bite-sized, as this will give your readers more to come back for. If I were talking about the house, I would break it down into various short how-to posts.

Note: For service-based businesses, I know your goal is not to tell everybody how to do everything (that's what they'll hire you for), but don't be afraid to give a little bit of something so that they can get started and know that they need to come to you for some more advanced topics.

Here's an example of a good How-To Post:

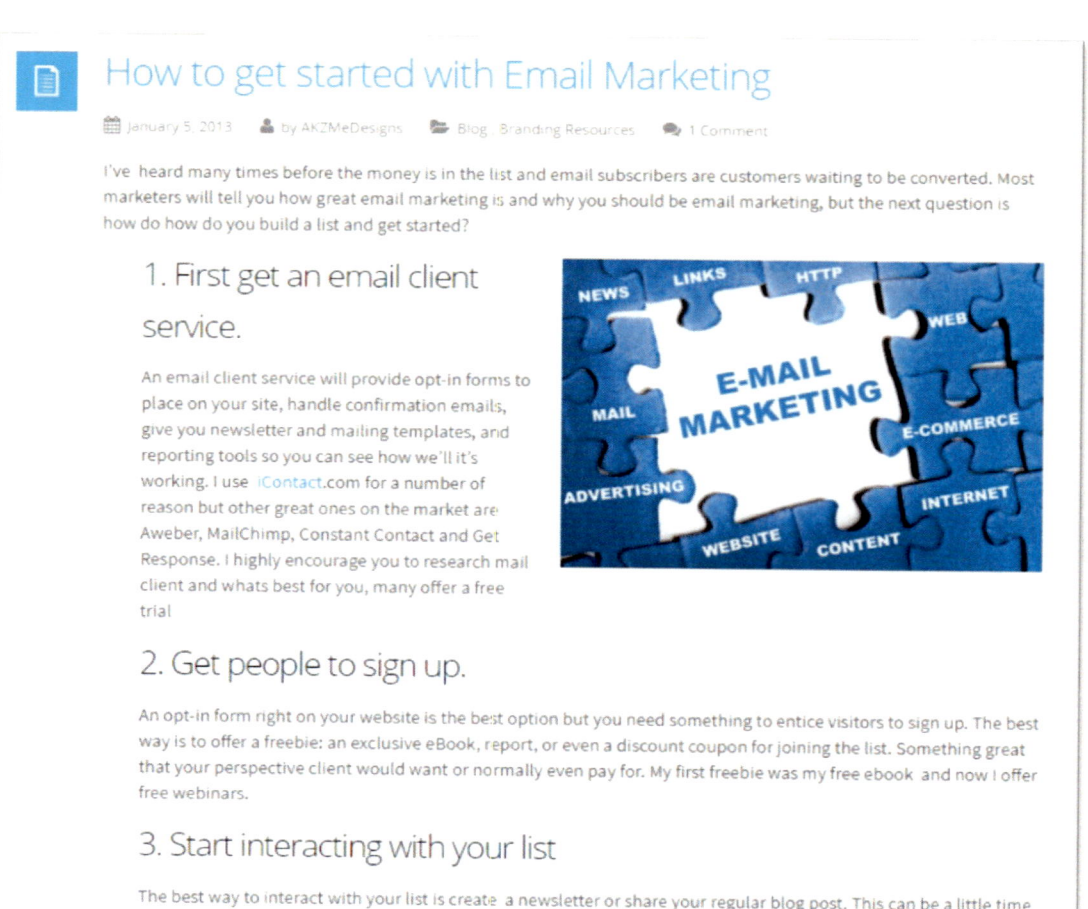

Review Post

Review posts are where you give your opinion on a product, a show, a book, etc. Anything that you can do a review of. In a review, I give my opinion, but I also give the pros and cons to help people form their own opinion. You can tell people what you thought about an event, the pros and cons, a few features and pricing. A really good review post may even bring in some other peoples' review of the item, so you get well-rounded opinions.

Here's an example of a review post:

Prestashop: Ecommerce Platform Review

Prestashop is an open-source e-commerce platform. It was founded back in 2007. It powers more than 165,000 online stores all over the world in 63 languages.

Features

Prestashop has more than 310 features and it comes with more than 3500 templates and modules. Here is a list of some of the major features of Prestashop.

- It comes with several marketing features including newsletters, coupons, loyalty programs, automatic email follow-ups, and many others.
- It comes with a complete analytic and reporting suite that makes reporting and analysis a piece of cake.
- It has more than 3500 templates and modules.
- Prestashop boosts the search engine ranking of the online store to a great extent.

Price

Since Prestashop is an open source platform, therefore, it is free to use. Prestashop is free to download and use. However, any add-on features that you choose aren't free for instance Amazon integration is priced $280 and MailChimp integration will cost you $200. Most of the templates are free but you will see that all the professional and decent templates aren't free.

Pros

- The biggest advantage of using Prestashop is that it is free

Interview Blog Post

An interview blog post is where you interview someone and share the commentary on your site. Most people do podcasts or video interviews, but there is still a lot of value in written interviews or getting the video or audio transcribed. You can interview customers, leaders in your industry, experts in other industries, anyone that you think can be of interest to your readers.

Interview posts are usually done in a question-and-answer format, so you can start with a few sentences about the person and their background and then continue with the questions.

> **TIP:** If you interview a well-known celebrity, use their name in the title to boost SEO traffic when people search for them. If you are interviewing a customer or just another expert (not as well known), use their title or what makes them stand out in the post title (example, Interview with a Trademark Expert). People are less likely to search for their name but will search for their expertise and keywords.

Here's a good example of an interview post:

Profile post

This is a little similar to an interview, but you're not actually going to talk to the person. A profile is written based on facts and information that is researched and known about the subject. The best example is Wikipedia – it's one big profile site. You can profile a person, company, event, etc., anything that people would be interested in learning more about and the background.

If you've ever seen the Goalcast videos, they are a lot like profile posts where you're just talking about someone's history, one of the struggles they went through, how they were raised, what impacted their results, and then some of the results that they got. That is a profile post.

Here's an example of Forbes' profile on Sheila Johnson:

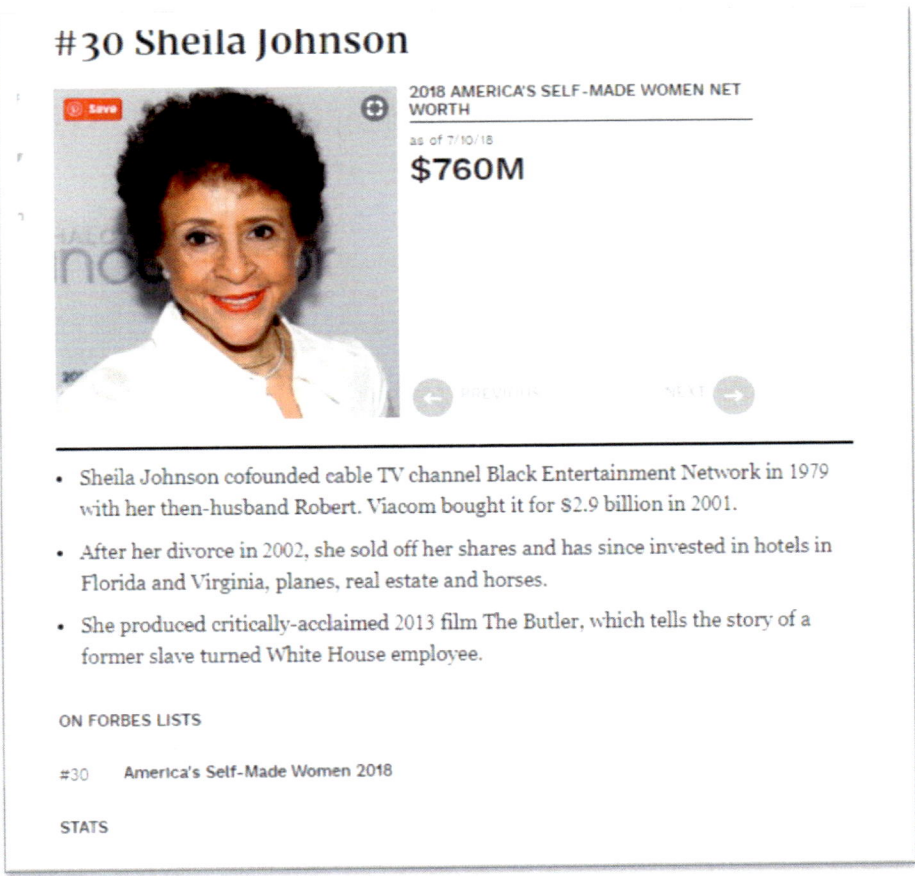

Comparison posts.

This is similar to your review post, but in your comparison post, you're going to compare two or more items to each other. The latest iPhone against the Note, comparing this camera to that camera, comparing this location to another location, or an organization to another organization. Anywhere you're putting two or more items up against each other.

If you're going to do a comparison post, I would recommend not doing more than four comparisons in one post; you don't want to overwhelm readers. If you want to do more than four, then I would maybe do a list post and just talk about each one separately. In a comparison post, you're going to probably go back and forth a little bit on it, comparing similar features

Here's a good example of a Comparison Post:

Case study

A case study is where you're talking about not just one particular person, but also a particular event and result they have. Most people use case studies to showcase how they helped a client receive very specific results. It's not an ad or testimonial but rather telling the story of the journey with the customer. Case studies are really great ways to showcase your clients, the results that they've gotten, and some of the skills that you put into making the change without being too salesy.

Ryan Deiss is the king of good case study examples on his site, www.digitalmarketer.com. Here's an example of one of the case studies:

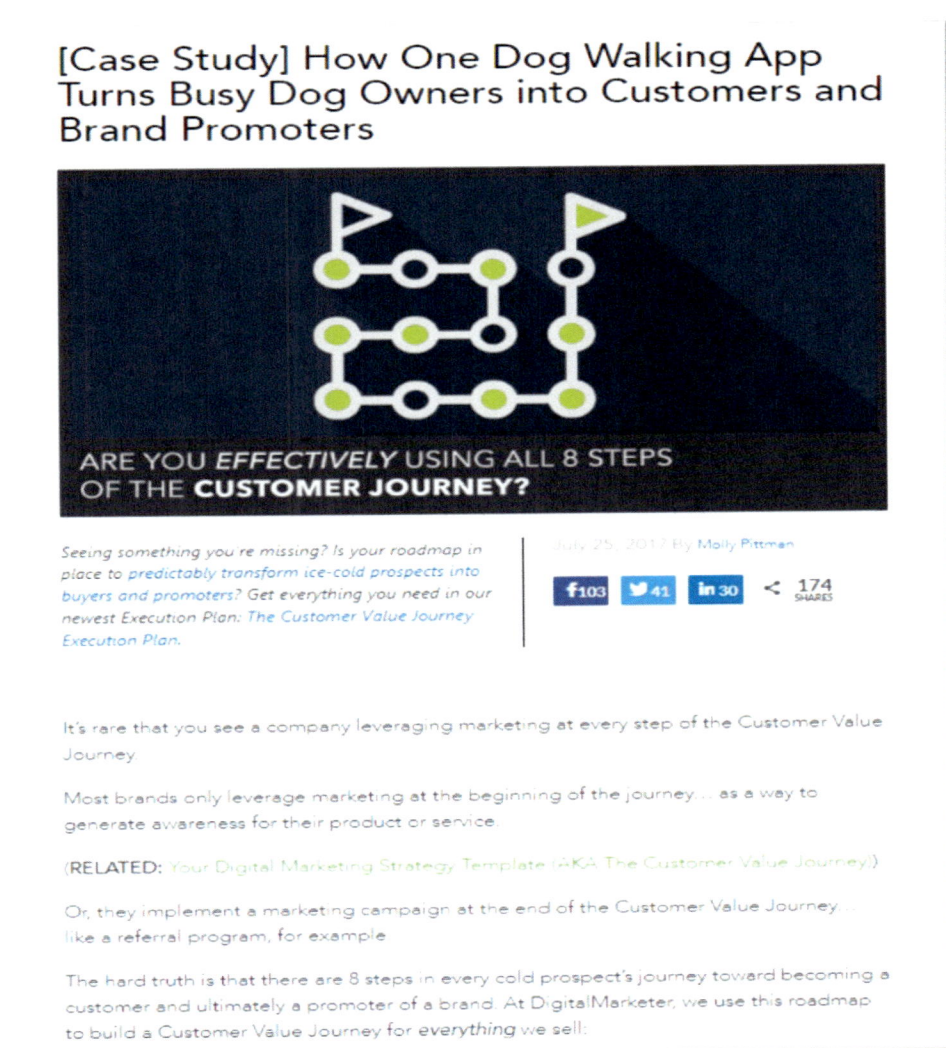

Link post

Link posts are a little bit similar to the list posts, but in this case, your whole goal is to link to others. We'll talk about that a lot in the next chapter about links. While it's natural to have a few links throughout all of your posts, the purpose of a link post is just to share links to other resources or sites. Many holiday gift guides are link posts because they give links to all of the products someone could purchase. Links in link posts could be to internal pages or external to other sites. List posts could also have links, and vice versa, but link posts are really just to link to other content.

Here's a list of latest and greatest articles from our members, how they are making blogging work for their businesses

Show them how to slay

Kierra at The KJones Collections slays the little black dress with hey piece on how to go from drab to fab with a few cute accessories. Readers love when you give ideas on how to make things they own already better.

http://www.thekjonescollection.com/blogs/style/143029255-7-ways-to-accessorize-a-black-dress

Get ready for fashion porn!!!!

Mikaela at Vetudejoy gives us everything with the Recap of her Fashion photo shoot trip to St. Thomas. Travel, fun, and fashion this is a Boutiquers dream come true and customer's fantasy. Showing customers "oh the places they can go" is great way to keep them thinking of you when they are making that list of things they love.

http://vetudejoy.com/blogs/news/97622150-travelinprints-st-thomas-with-renae-bluitt-and-vetu-de-joy

Out with the old and in with the new

Hannah at Nola Rae Boutique gives us a great example of blog post that is about more than just selling. Every post doesn't have to be product product product, sometimes post just help your readers out.

https://www.nolaraeboutique.com/blogs/5-easy-steps-to-spring-clean-your-closet/

Opinion piece

An opinion post is great for sharing your thoughts, and this post is purely dedicated to you giving your views on a topic. Usually, it's more of an editorial, not a review, and on social media, this would be a RANT. Opinion posts are a great chance for you to show off your authority in your space, as you can state your argument and support your opinion with facts and stats that really show you know your stuff. This is your chance to be the CNN commentator and give your opinion on what's going on.

Here's an example of an opinion post I did on a great debate on online video:

Facebook or YouTube? Where should you put your videos for the best SEO results

As part of my "No Content Left" behind push this weekend. I grabbed a bunch of my Live videos from Facebook and made them into blog post (You've probably read a few)...

...and the big thing I pulled a bunch of videos and put them on YOUTUBE!!!!

Yes, YouTube

Someone in my groups asked why put them on YouTube and not share from Facebook?

Good question...

Most people don't know how important YouTube is for your SEO

Some of the one-off blog posts I embed from Facebook. But for a page like the Video page, I created YouTube is the #winner if you want to boost your search engine positions (aka rankings)

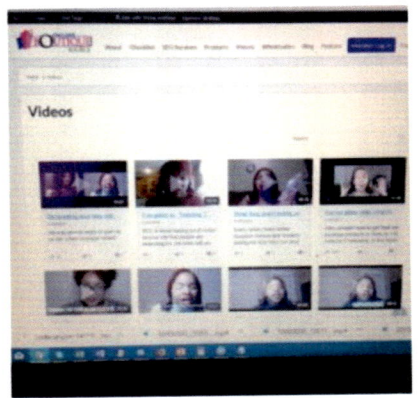

Here are few reasons:

Story Post

Telling stories helps you connect with your audience and show the human side of your site and business. It could be a story about how you got started, or about a struggle you're going through. Think of those epic Instagram posts where you're really pouring out your heart and turn it into a cost with a business lesson in the end. You can even tell a story about someone else, about some industry leader, about a client. Making story posts are mostly about building a connection and making it real for your audience.

Gathering Posts

Gathering posts are where you're pretty much pulling together information from a bunch of different sources and putting in one post to help your audience find the answers they need. It's like when you did term papers and text papers in college. You had to do all of the research, and name your sources, and synthesize some of the information; this is what a gathering post would do.

Here's an example of a post I did on taxes for online retailers:

US Sales Tax and your Online Boutique

Understanding sales tax is a very important part of selling online. Many believe that since they created their store online that they don't have to worry about sales tax. This isn't true and unfortunately many online boutique owners get burned because of forgotten tax payments.

US sales tax is tax collected on the sale or lease of goods or services. The tax is calculated by multiplying the price charged on the goods or services purchased or leased. Each state has it's own sales tax rates. This tax is usually imposed on brick and mortar businesses with a physical storefront. It's also imposed in brick and mortar businesses with an online store.

How US sales tax is collected

States require that businesses charge buyers the sales tax at the time of sale. That is, the tax is added to the purchase price. The businesses are then required to remit the collected taxes at the time in which they file their tax returns. In general, this tax is charged only once. However, in instances where a good or service is sold more than once as in the case of second hand goods, the tax might be charged more than once.

Does the US sales tax apply to online stores and boutiques?

Currently, the sales tax only applies to online businesses with a physical presence in a particular state. States also have the authority to collect sales tax from retailers operating in other places. This leaves out retailers that sell their products exclusively online. However, a bill that's yet to be passed in Congress aims at changing this.

How do you define physical presence?

These are the most popular blogs post types. As you can see, with so many ways to write a blog post, it's easy to add a variety and keep interest on your site.

When you put your topic and type together, you can mix and match these to make 100s of posts. You could do a question topic and put it as a review. Somebody could have a question like, "what's the best camera to use for live stream videos?" and you could answer on your site in a review blog post style.

When you use your keywords with these first two steps of the content process, you'll create an amazing blog post that does well in search, keeps people coming to your site, and helps you keep your SEO-ranking factors up.

My SEO Workbook

EXERCISE

To help you organize your blog content, in this exercise, we'll combine the work we've done in the last two chapters. Complete the worksheet with the keyword, category, topic, and type. This list can be your final content list.

Reminder: It's best to create content in groups, so I've organized a workshop by category, then keyword, and for each keyword, five lines for topics to create.

Category	
Keyword	
Topic	**Type**

Keyword	
Topic	**Type**

Keyword	
Topic	**Type**

STEP 3: Post it

Now that we've talked about the different types of topics and what we can write on our site, how it's time to publish it online. The post-it step is about the structure and semi-technical part of posting your blog posts.

I follow a simple writing structure:

Intro

- Catch phrase or questions letting readers know what the post is about and why it helps them

Core content

- This is the meat and potatoes of the post where I use subtitle, list, stories to make the main part of the post

Summary

- This is where I round things up, I'll restate the main points and what they learned from the post.

Call to Action

- The CTA is where you tell somewhat to do next. We're blogging for business so you want to lead to something a link to click, a download or opt in to get more information, set up a call to discuss, or even chat about it in your groups. 90% of your content should have a next step that leads closer to you. Usually I have my CTA at the end but sometimes, I'll squeeze in the middle or beginning or even say it more the once

There are lot of writing structures but this is the quickest and works well for most blog types.

Another part of the Post it step are the headings, tags, and code that we covered in Chapter 6. The buttons you push will be different, based on your website platform, but the underlying code and structure should be the same for search engines to pick it up correctly.

To recap from chapter 6 here's the diagram of the components each post should have

EXERCISE

Let's map out a Post

In this exercise, take 1 of the post we've chosen to write from step 2 and filling all of the parts using the Intro, Core, Summary structure I shared and adding the SEO tags we need to make this a perfect SEO post. You don't have to write the post word for word the idea here is to jot down your thoughts so you have all of the major components covered

I set up 1 here. But copy and repeat this for each post

Title		
Intro		
Core	Sub topic 1	
	Sub topic 2	
	Sub topic 3	
	Bullets (if applicable)	
	Supporting Story	
Hyperlinks		
Summary		
Call to action		
Image and Image tags		
Page description		
Category		Meta tags	

Copyright 2018

How Much Should I Write

Before we wrap up our content chapters, I want to talk a little bit about the length of the content.

In 2017, the average number of words for pages and blogs that were showing up on page one was 1,800 words. So, when you're thinking about your blog content, Google likes meatier content that really digs in, answers the question, and gives the information. This also gives you more room for keywords and more things that people can search on.

Don't skim on the words for blog posts.

Google reads all content and words on your page, but you have a slight advantage if you have more words and content. Remember, Google wants to give people the best answers possible, so if one page goes into a lot of details while your site only has a brief overview, the detail has a better chance of being #1. More words also help with your users' readability, giving them more value and establishing your site as an expert resource.

The good news is everything doesn't have to be a long, major blog post. Depending on what you're writing and the type of page, you have a little flexibility in how many words you'll want on the page. Here's a brief rundown of your pages and recommends length.

An average blog post is between 700 to 1,000 words. I won't go less than a 500-word blog post. This gives you enough words to make a point and provide examples or stories to get you up to those numbers.

Epic blog post (sometimes called guides) is another style of blog post that is meant to go really deep into a topic. Epic blog posts give a lot of detail examples, sometimes instruction, and often are a combination of 2–3 of the types we talked about above. An epic blog post can be over 2,000 words, but you want at least 1,500, especially if blogging isn't your business.

Show notes are the posts that you use to accompany your podcasts and videos. Show notes are written to give an overview of what is in the audio content, and these can be a little bit shorter, somewhere between 300 to 500 words per post.

Product Descriptions should be a little bit shorter than most pages. We've talked about the product description formula, and you want to make a big impact with only a few words to describe your products. I wouldn't go more than 100–150 words for a product description. Although there are probably lots of things you can share, you still want to keep it bite-sized and consumable for the reader, and for the usability aspect of it.

About and Services pages can be the same length, 300 to 500. Unless you're doing a longer (sales page-like) service page, a few hundred words should be enough. We talked about doing a services page and then breaking down into a smaller services page. If you have multiple services or a lot of information that you're sharing, then you can do a little bit longer.

Case studies can be on the long side, 1000 or words similar to epic posts. The goal is to really tell the story and share the results with a good case study. You don't have to give all of the how but going a little bit deep into the different steps that made the solution work will make a good case study.

Homepage varies based on the type of site that you have. I would at least try to make sure I have 20 to 30 words for my retailers or people with more photos and videos on their homepage, up to 100 if you're really starting to get into who you serve, what you serve, and how you serve them on your homepage. Your homepage does not need to have a lot of words and content, but you want to make sure that it does hit those points that we talked about in the earlier section.

In summary, Google likes words. Google likes a meatier, wordy post, but you also want to balance it with how much your user is going to read and learn. If you're just writing words to write the words, then I would say, just have fewer words. This is a guideline. It's not a requirement. It's not going to tell you, "No, this is a bad post," or "Google's going to reject it completely if it's a short post." I just know that you have better chances of ranking higher if you have a good number of words on your site.

BUTTTTT I don't want to Blog

Now that we've done all of this talk about how to blog, I know there are still a lot of people are like, "Well, I don't want to blog."

Don't worry I got you.

It's important for me to let you know that there are other ways to put content on your site, even if you don't blog. However, a blog is still one of the most effective ways to get your SEO quickly, which is why we have about 20 pages on just blogging.

But blogging is only a name, just because you're "blogging," putting regular posts on your site, doesn't mean it has to have a date and a time or be called a blog. Blogging is just a name; I want you to focus on creating content, not making it into a blog.

Podcast

A podcast is an audio file that you would put up on a site like iTunes and Stitcher, but you also want to have a version of that file on your site. Most podcasts are accompanied by show notes. Show notes are a brief summary on your site that tells what the episodes are about,

about the guest, important links discussed in the episode, and any other information you want to share. You can use the topics strategies we discussed in the last chapter to choose podcast topics for your site and use relevant keywords in your show notes.

> **TIP:** Another really important thing you can do with show notes, is if you have guests, you can also incorporate their names and their keywords into your show notes. This is going to help you get found for not just your content, but also a little bit for them as well. I have a post that gets found continuously because I have a pretty high-profile guest who gets searched a lot, and so they find the episode.

Video

Video, similar to a podcast, you want to give an overview of what's in it. You'll see in some of my videos, I put a little intro, the video itself, and then a couple of bullet points of what they would have learned. In the video, I like to put what questions would have been answered, what topics would have been covered, keeping in mind some of the things we just talked about in the blog and pulling those out, and keeping in mind my keywords. That's what you want to be on these pages.

Resource pages

Resources pages offer places you can get information about different topics that are important to your industry. These resources pages can be whatever information you want to provide:

- list of important terms
- links to other organizations
- books that can be helpful
- supplies that are useful
- Directory of providers

Anything that can be a resource to readers; the beauty is you don't have to add new information like on a blog. My past sickle cell client, they had a resource page with different resources and bullets to other sickle cell foundations, sickle cell studies, sickle cell information. This page helped them top rank#6 for sickle cell foundations.

Profile and interview series. Profiles and interviews are one of the blog types we discussed, but you can also have these as a stand-alone section on your site with or without a blog. Just like resources pages, you don't have to add news on a regular basis, and just like the podcast, you can leverage the guest keywords and search presence too. I've seen people just have nothing but profiles, interviews, case studies.

News and Updates

News and Updates are a place where you share some of the happenings, goings-on updates in your industry or business. I use this a lot for my community-based and organization sites. A news section has a lot of trending post that lets you give information based on what's happening at the time. Similar to newspapers, these sites get a lot of traffic when people search for historical references. An example would be, on my site, I can do a section on just the latest SEO updates, or things like that.

All of these options are considered content. At the end of the day, Google is going to index and find anything you put on your site, so don't stress if it's not a formal blog.

You can use these ideas to put additional content aside from your Home page, About page, Services page. The more content you have, the better your chances of getting found and getting found faster in search.

When all else fails hire someone

My last tip on blog is outsource. Unless you're a write or a blogger there is nothing that says you have created all of your content yourself. Aside from get guest bloggers for your whole site there are other outsource options

Hire a staff or Ghost writer- there are sites where you can hire writers

- iwriter
- Upwork
- Problogger Job Boards
- OnlineJob.ph
- Fiverr
- I hire an intern

Transcribe your words- I use a few services to take the words I speak and turn them into post

- Rev.com
- Temi
- Google Docs Speech function
- Hire a transcriber on fiverr or Up work

The Ranking Checklist

1) Initial site checks
   - ✓ Confirm Google analytics access (Chapter 2)
   - ✓ Confirm Google search console (Chapter 2)
   - ✓ Get Current Metrics (Chapter 2)
   - ✓ Do initial site readiness checks (Chapter 4)
     - ✓ 404 errors
     - ✓ Address URL issues
     - ✓ Blank descriptions
     - ✓ Duplicate content
     - ✓ Broken links
     - ✓ Blank alt tags
2) Complete keyword research (Chapter 5)
   - ✓ Round Up- Create list of potential keywords
   - ✓ Analyze- Check volume and competition for keywords
   - ✓ Connect- Create a potential list of topics and categories
   - ✓ Engage- Test your words out in post and on social
   - ✓ Select 5-10 focus keywords
3) Update Content on site
   - ✓ Add keywords to pages on your site (Chapter 6)
   - ✓ Find Update images (Chapter 6)
   - ✓ Update page tags, descriptions, headings, images, etc. (Chapter 6)
   - ✓ Choose SEO friendly topics (Chapter 7)
   - ✓ Choose blog post types you like (Chapter 7)
   - ✓ Write 5-10 blog post (Chapter 7)
4) Internal inks (Chapter 8)
   - ☐ Identify pages without links
   - ☐ Identify pages to link to on your site
   - ☐ Create internal links
6) External Linking (Chapter 8)
   - ☐ Find link building opportunities
   - ☐ Fid group to collaborate with
   - ☐ Monitor incoming links
7) Wrap up and ongoing (Chapter 9)
   - ☐ Schedule future blog post
   - ☐ Pitch link building opportunities
   - ☐ Update target keywords
   - ☐ Complete Monthly Look back and plan ahead
   - ☐ Monthly 2-4 blog post with internal link
   - ☐ Monthly 5-10 backlinks

Chapter 8 The Power of the Link

Google online loves you when everyone else loves you first. - WendyPiersall

Now that we've got amazing SEO ready content on our site, there is one more step that is going to put our SEO above all of the other wanna-be rankers out there.

This is my favorite part and the last piece of the SEO pie, **POPULARITY**!!! I'll also like to call this the **secret sauce** of SEO, and the reason why I call it the secret sauce is because it's the thing that really makes SEO work and makes Google look at your site differently, compared to another site. It's also the thing that people forget the most when they build their sites or work on SEO. You know how when you go to a restaurant, they have regular chicken with just a little fancy sauce on top that makes it amazing? The secret is in the sauce, and the sauce for SEO is link building, particularly backlinking. In this chapter, we'll talk all about the links and how you can get lots of secret sauce.

Google and SEO work like a bit of a popularity contest. Like in high school where you have the captain of the football team, everyone knows him and loves his name because he's connected to the coaches, the team, the teachers, the newspapers, other teams they play, etc. He's really popular because the sport he plays has a lot of people connecting with him. Then you have the captain of the chess team who may not have as many team members, fans, never recognized by the local papers, small game, one coach. He may have connections but not as many or as prominent as the football captain. As a result, fewer people know the chess captain's name, and he's not as popular.

That is SEO backlinks! The more connections and popularity your site has, the better you'll do in the search ranks.

So in this chapter, we're going to talk all about creating links. We're going to talk about creating internal links, backlinks, the dos and don'ts of link building, and things to understand when you are creating links, because they're really, really important.

The power of the link

Search engines see every page as a separate entity; the site domain name shows they are related, but it's really the hyperlinks between the pages that lets search engines know they are connected and connects them to outside sites. The world wide web is really a web.

Links are great, but every link is not created equal. Links carry **Link Juice**, and link juice is determined by the rank of the originating page. If a page is doing well in the search ranking, then any pages that link to it is going to get a little bit of credibility from the page.

It's like the 90's movie *Juice* with Tupac, where whoever did the most and had the most street cred had "the juice," and by default, their friends had a little juice too.

With this in mind, if you get bigger and more popular sites to link, you get a bit of link juice. The more sites and the larger the sites, the better your page will rank.

Creating a beautiful link

In the next sections, we'll talk about where to get links and what links look like and creating links that get you better SEO traction.

Links are hyperlinks on our page that when clicked, lead to another page or site. You can link via text, images, buttons, and menus. Most sites button and menus are set up by the platform, so I'm not going to go into them that much, but I want to focus on the text links.

There are two important parts to the link:

1. **Anchor text:** anchor text are the words visible on the screen that the link is attached to – this is the part you can see. The anchor text gives Search engines an idea of what the link is about.
2. **Target link** is the URL the link takes you to when clicked – the part you can't see. This is where the link juice will go the most.

Most people put the "name" or "click here" for their anchor text, and they point to the home page as the target. This is actually bad for SEO. Saying click here or just the site's name doesn't give a good idea of what the link is about and leading to your home page doesn't give link juice to your content pages that will get better rankings.

For the best links, when possible, you want to use a phrase and/or your keywords as the anchor text and target a link to a specific page or post on your site.

Here's a little grid to help you make the prettiest links:

	Anchor	Target Link
BAD	Click Here	www.yoursite.com
BAD	Yoursite.com or name	www.yoursite.com
GOOD	Best <insert keyword> business	www.yoursite.com
GOOD	Yoursite.com or name	www.yoursite.com/specific_page
BEST	**Best <insert keyword> business**	**www.yoursite.com/specific_page**

Two types of links

Internal links, aka Spread the Love

Internal links are links within your site link from one page to another. Your menu, footer and sidebars all are internal links, but you also can make internal links within your post and content. Your complete control of internal links gives you the opportunity to create the connections you want within your site. Most sites I review have very few links within their site, but I recommend every post to have three to four links. Most of my pages with content, except for my services page, also have at least three to four links. The reason why I don't put as many on my services page is because I want people to stay on that page for as long as possible. I don't want readers going out and finding other things when the next step is to sign up for a service, but on other pages: FAQ pages, resource pages, blog post pages, about page, I link away.

> **HINT:** Overall, you want to have at least three to four links per post, per page. If you have a longer post, like an epic blog post that's over 1500 words, then you can have more internal links a little bit more and do five to six per post.

What this does is it helps to spread the link juice love throughout the site. You may have one post became really popular and a lot of external sites linked to. As a result, it's got the Juice, and by putting a few links to other pages on the page, you're spreading the love and letting Google know the other pages have good content too.

Internal links are also good for usability. You know how many times I have gone to Wikipedia and clicked on somebody's link on the page, then clicked on somebody else's name from that link, then clicked on another. 30 mins later, I'm still on in a Wiki rabbit hole; that's what you want people to do on your site – spend hours consuming content this helps with the time on site and pages visited ranking factors we talked about, early in the book.

WARNING: I know it may be tempting to go link-crazy and link all over to every product and service you have, but be careful that the links make sense to your visitors too. Keep it relevant and related.

My SEO Workbook

EXERCISE

For this exercise, I want you to start looking at opportunities to create links within your site. I want you to fill out this little diagram of links that you can build. Start with your most popular post (you can pull from the pages and posts we optimized in chapter 6). Look for the pages that are getting most traffic right now, and which are already ranking.

Put the page name in the first box. Then read through the page and identify three pages you can create links to (bonus: if it's also one of your top pages). Do this for two levels of pages, and even link some back to other post after a while, you will see how your site starts forming its own web.

Use this exercise to go through and start creating what will be the links of your site. I'm only giving you a couple of boxes here, but I want you to make a point to go and link through your entire site. There are some extra linking pages in the back of the book to help you with continuing the exercise.

Example: If a post is about dresses. You may put something in there, and you may have to add a sentence, so you may have to say, "Another great item that you can use prints really well is on your shirts," and maybe you might link to your shirts. In your products themselves, in your product descriptions for retailers, you can link to other items that may go well with this outfit or go well with the piece. If you have a necklace, earrings that will also go well with this. It's also a good way to boost your sales, hint, hint.

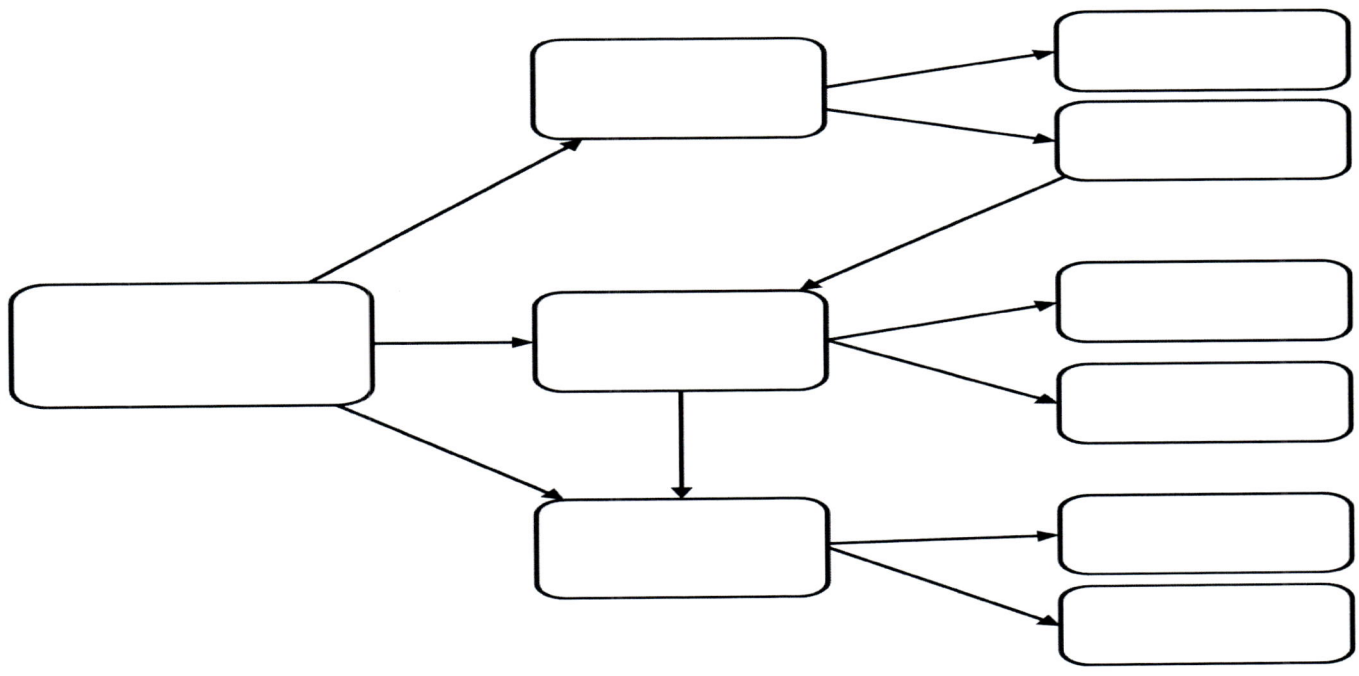

External Links, aka Backlinks

The next thing we want to consider is backlinks. Backlinks are links from other sites to your site. This is what Brian Dean of Backlinko has really made his entire career, blog, and everything on – how to get really good backlinks – it's that big of a deal. Backlinks are a little bit tricky because you don't control who links to you. You have to ask other people to link to your site, and/or create amazing content that people just want to link to.

Backlinks can be in the form of a guest post where they link to your name, an interview where they link to your site, or your name, or something like that. It can also be a quote. Or, if you know a business that's complementary to yours. For example, I had two clients with similar audiences at the same time; one did restaurant websites, the other one did Facebook Ads. When I created their content, I did an article about marketing on the restaurant website's blog. In the article, I mentioned people should use Facebook Ads, and I linked to the client who did Facebook Ads. On another site when I wrote about websites designs, I linked to the web design client. I'm fortunate that I sometimes have related clients that I can link to each other, but this isn't always the case.

In Google's mind, backlinking happens all organically. People see your site, they love your stuff, and they link to you. While that does happen occasionally, it's few and far between, and if I told you to wait around for unicorn links in this book, you'd be pretty mad and ready to throw the book at me (pun intended).

So instead, I am going to give you 10 different ways that you can reach out to get backlinks to your site; that will speed up backlinking and still look really natural to Google and other search engines. There are pros and cons to each of these strategies, so for each one, I'll give the pros, cons, and how you can do it.

Podcast

Podcasts are one of my favorite ways to get backlinks (I talk a lot, LOL). Podcasts help you in two ways; 1. More people will learn about you and your expertise, 2. You get a backlink for SEO, and your name has more results will people google you.

Pros:

- Podcasts take the least prep work and writing.
- The podcast host does all of the work, you just show up and be fabulous.
- You can do a lot of shows in a short period of time.

Cons:

- You have to pitch a lot to get on shows.
- In the beginning, you'll get a lot of rejections because you aren't well-known but keep pushing; some shows love to have newcomers and unique stories.
- Podcasts are great for steady links coming in, but if you need them quickly, this may be an issue. You have to wait for the podcast host to publish the episode. I've waited months for some shows to be published and show up in search.

How you can get these links:

When I look for podcasts to pitch to, I look for podcasts that are within my niche, have a similar audience, and they write show notes and put links on their site. Not everyone with a podcast put the information on their site website, so it's important to double check this.

HINT: When I pitch a show, I'll usually propose three titles that I think will fit their audience. Use your keyword and topics research to create three titles that fit your SEO profile. This can help the interviews you do on other sites also rank for your keywords, which builds your authority when people search and see a page full of you speaking on the subject.

Guest Blog Posts

A guest blog post is when you write a full blog post for someone else. It's not salesy or about you; it's a post where you're sharing some piece of your expertise. An example, http://onlineboutiquesource.com/friends-business-partners, is that when I wanted to talk about a legal topic on my site instead of writing myself, I asked my lawyer friend, Merissa Grayson, to write a post. She wrote a full guest post on creating partnerships in your business. In the post, I listed her as the author and linked to her site, her information.

Guest blog posts have to be original content you write for the site. Once you write a post, you should not put the same post on your site or another site. You can discuss the same topic on different sites but put a little spin on each, so it's not duplicate content. Just like you do with the podcast, the best way to pitch the guest blog post is to look on peoples' sites to see if they have guest blog posts and have an audience that you can give insight from your experience.

Pros

- Guest blog posts will definitely share your expertise with the world
- Guest blog posts get you in front of new audiences.
- The post will last for years and years to come. I have posts I wrote back and 2012 out there still linking to my sites

Cons

- It's A LOT of writing.
- This strategy works as much as you do. Unless you're a writer, creating unique content could become overwhelming, but still give it a try, getting a good 20-30 post out on the web could be a great boost for your online presence.

How you can get these links:

A good way to find sites that are looking for guest writers is to Google your keywords, plus "guest blog post," "guest blog," "guest writer" and you'll find people who are actively looking for guest blog posts or have introduced a guest writer in the past.

> **TIP:** Another hint when I'm examining sites to pitch is, I look for medium-sized sites that have been around for at least a year. I also use SEMrush to see if they have a little SEO standing too, which mean they will likely have a little link juice

BONUS: On the resource site http://onlineboutiquesource.com/seobookresources I'll give you my pitch template, so you can reach out to people to get on podcasts, guest posts, whatever you can get on.

Awards and Recognitions

Another way of getting links are awards and recognitions, such as "Top…." list. Top lists are those posts you see people share a lot when they are highlighted as the top of something, like "Top Influencers in 2019," "Best gifts for 2019," etc. Most time, we're just excited to get your name out there and that you're on the list for something, but what you may not know is you've all just scored a big SEO win, which will last much longer than the year of the list. Usually, when people create these list or list awardees for their event, the list also contains a link to the site, a backlink.

Pro:

- These lists boost your SEO and your credibility at the same time.
- They are also a great ego boost.
- Asking to be recognized is a great way to practice being unapologetically you.

Cons:

- Most lists only happen one time a year
- you'll need to keep looking for new lists and opportunities.

How you can get these links:

Best way to get on those top lists is showing up in your industry and making sure that people who've done lists in the past know who you are. Also applying for awards whenever you see them come up, even if you know a past awardee. Usually, if someone does a list for one year (i.e., 2017), they will do the same for the following year (i.e., 2018). Research lists that highlight business in your industry and email or tweet at them to let them know that your site would be a good fit for the next year's list.

Quotes

Quote backlinks are when someone references a few words or sentences you've said on your site and then attribute with your name and link.

Pros:

- Quotes are the easiest backlinks because all you have to do is say a few words or sentences about your expertise.
- Quotes help position you as an expert to the reader
- You can reference that you were quoted in your own marketing.

Cons:

- The hard part of this strategy is looking for people who need quotes.
- People may use the quote and list your name but not backlink to your site (make sure you ask for a link up front).

How you can get these links:

I approach this in two ways: 1) I'll email blogs with similar audience and people who have written about topics I can discuss and offer a quote or link to help add more to their existing articles, 2) I'll respond to inquiries in blogging groups or on twitter where people are looking for experts or information on a specific topic.

Another resource to research people looking for quotes is **Help a Reporter Out** (HARO). HARO is a daily email service that contains people looking for expert opinions. Only problem I have with HARO is sometimes, the source will not create a link to your site. They may put your name and website in the post, but they don't give the hyperlink, which is what we need for SEO. While I like Help a Reporter Out, I think it's really good for PR and getting yourself out there. It's only but so great for SEO.

Last way to get quotes is using collaborations. If a group of business owners each have a site, it is a great time to see where and how you can quote each other or reference someone's content.

Be an Authority with a unique approach

This is a strategy piggybacking off of Brian Dean's Skyscraper Technique. The skyscraper technique is when you write about a new strategy or concept for your industry, give it a catchy name, and as people find out about the new technique, they link to your site as the original source. For example, when we talked about keywords, I've originated the R.A.C.E. method, this is something that is new and different to the industry. Although people do and teach keyword research, they haven't broken it done into a quick 4-part strategy that makes keyword research easy for even the SEO novice like the R.A.C.E. method. As more people read and learn this technique, I become the "skyscraper," aka tallest building, and what happens if you are the tallest building in an area? A lot of people start to point to you, talking about you, looking at you.

> PRO: This strategy can really raise your visibility and credibility, because not only are you sharing super valuable information, but you are also positioning yourself as a pioneer in your space.
>
> Con: This can be one of the slowest ways to get backlinks, as a lot of this method is dependent on if people find, like, and reference your content. You may not even know when people are linking to you, at first; you'll just find it during your SEO tracking.

How you can get these links:

The best way to find your own skyscraper is to think of the things you've got a special system or a special name for and write about it to share with the world. This may be one of your secret sauce or tips you use to really help your customers. In this tip, give just a little away to help get the name out there. A good example is my friend Kim McCarter. A few years ago, she introduced the Beyoncé Funnel, which is a sales funnel strategy she mapped out based on how Beyoncé was selling concert tickets. Now, if you Google 'Beyoncé Funnel,' you will see all kinds of references to Kim and the Beyoncé Funnel. You may have a different way that you pair your prints with your stripes, you may have a different way or different method that you use to clean the house, or do some type of cleaning activity, you may have a different way that you make chicken, or you do recipes, a healthy recipe. All those can be your form of the Skyscraper Technique.

One way to help this strategy move a little bit faster than normal is to help people pick up your content; share it on social media, email it to notable people in your niche, tweet about it often, go live about it, mention it in your interviews, if you see somebody asking questions, you can answer in a group and share the link with them, etc. Do everything you can to make your thing a bigger thing, LOL. This is where you can use social media to help get your links out there more, and hopefully, to help people to link to you more.

Badges and Affiliates

Badges were very popular on sites a few years ago. You would see blogs with BlogHer or Blogalicious images all over their sites, but what many did not know (or they knew and were ok with it) is that those badges with links were also backlinks and really good for SEO. Today, people use badges less, but they often have affiliates or host events that would have people link to their site.

Affiliates links and badges give people an incentive to link to you, either they are links to make a profit, or they are linking to you because showing the image boosts their credibility (like wearing brand names in the 90s); either way, it's a win-win for everyone. This is the original online influencer marketing, LOL.

So, if you have affiliates to your site or you have hosted a conference and gave people little images to say they were a speaker and link to you, then you have backlinks. YAY!!!

Pro:

- If you have a good incentive, people will run to post your links.
- In addition to the SEO benefit, you'll also get an increase in direct traffic from people clicking the link.

Cons:

- Creating an event or affiliate program can be a lot of work up front.
- You'll have to pay a percentage of your profits if you have an affiliate program.
- People may remove the badges and links after a while.

How to get these links?

You can create something that people will want to put the badge on their site. Speaker badges are always the easiest, but you have to host a conference, telesummit, etc. to get the speakers on.

NOTE: the affiliate links must contain your site's name to get the SEO benefit. If you are using a 3rd party tool like SamCart to manage affiliates, the links created will not result in backlinks.

Feature people on your site

Just like Badges and Affiliates, this is another way to entice people to your site by giving them an incentive. Profile, interviews, podcast and list posts are great blog post types to talk about a person or their business. Often when people are featured on a site, they'll put a link to the post on their own site, which gives you a backlink.

Pros:

- You'll be creating great content for your site and getting backlinks at the same time.
- Features are also a good way to connect with influencers (people love when you talk about them).

Cons:

- This method isn't a guaranteed link, like the affiliates and badges. There are some people who will get featured and not mention it on their site.

How to get these links?

Just start writing about people. The good news is you don't need permission to write about someone, as long as what you are saying is true and you're not using their original content like music, copyrighted videos, etc. You can write about people as much as you like. Most find it flattering and are happy to be featured. Once you've written about the people, send them an email, DM or tweet, letting them know they've been featured.

To increase the chances of getting a backlink to your feature, look for people who have a medium-sized following and who aren't featured a lot. For Example, Cardi B IS NOT going to give you a backlink, but her sister who doesn't get as much attention might respond. Also, review their website before you write the feature and see if they have a page where they list sites and shows they've been on and/or if they write a separate post when they are featured.

Testimonials

When was the last time you shouted out to your favorite product, service provider, or coach? That shout-out or praise could get you a backlink. Many companies (especially B2B) look for testimonials or reviews about their products and services, and when they post these, they put the names and links of the sites.

Pros:

- It's usually quick and easy to give a testimonial, doesn't take a lot of time or effort
- It's a way to show support for the product and people you like

Cons

- The products audience may differ from your core audience.
- Not all sites make the links active in their testimonials

How to get these links?

Check out the sites for the tools and services you already use. If they have testimonials with links, reach out and let them know how much you love their product and you would like to do a testimonial. Most companies like testimonials that stand out, so if you have a story of how you got great results or a unique way you've been using their tool, then you are more likely to be selected for the testimony.

Directories

Directories are a list of links to sites, similar to an online yellow pages phone book. They usually offer very little information about the sites and just list their names and links. I almost left this option out of this book because it has gotten such a bad rap over the years and Google is really critical of this type of sites because so many list spammy links and use them to get backlinks quickly, but I like to be thorough and didn't want you to wonder why it wasn't here, so here it is.

Directories aren't all bad, and while some are just long list of sites, some are associated with a specific location, service, or group, which make them really valuable resources. For example, the local chamber of commerce, vending events, and organizations with licensed vendors often have directories that are great reference tools for searchers.

Pros

- Directories are usually very easy to find. Google directory and your niche, location, or other attributes, and there may be a directory for it.
- They are easy to get into, there isn't much of a criterion or limited number which can be listed
- Some specific directories are frequently searched by visitors looking for sites and resources in that area.

Cons

- Directories are big targets for search engines' algorithm changes. So, many people have abused them that they are one of the first places google looks at for spammy links.
- Many directories have a cost. Because they are so easy to get listed, people will charge a fee to be listed in a directory. Even the legitimate lists may require regular fees or membership to be listed (don't ignore because there is a fee; these are often the most beneficial sites).
- Some directories will have no-follow links that do now share their link juice, and to avoid being a target by Google, some directories have changed how their links appear to the search engine.

How to get these links?

Research different directories: 1) look on Google and your local areas for directories that are a good fit for your business 2) look for directories that list your competitors (you should be there too) 3) ask organizations and associations you are part of, if they have a directory of vendors or members. Once you've located a few directories, review their submission criteria and follow instructions for submission.

TIP: Free directories can take months to list your site, but if it's a paid directory, try to get a timeline for when new submissions will show up.

Collaboration

The easiest way to get links is through collaborations. We spend a lot of time connecting online but rarely utilize for a long-term benefit to our business. I always say this, especially for my ladies (sorry fellas), we naturally do a lot of connecting and talking to each other on social media, but we very rarely take that connect to our websites where we get a greater ROI. Many of the activities on the list can also be used for collaborations. For example;

- You can appear on your biz friend's podcast
- You can guest blog post for another friend's site
- You can provide a quote as an expert on a site
- You can be interviewed or profiled

All of these things you can do with people you're already connected to.

For example, instead of linking to a big-name industry guru as a reference in a post, you can link to somebody you know and have firsthand experience with their ability.

In my SEO membership, we have a weekly linking thread. We're asking; *anybody need a link? Anybody writing about something that they can collaborate with someone else?* Collaboration is really one of the easiest because you don't have to do a lot of extra reaching out; you just have to talk to people. If you're already doing that, you could already be getting links.

Along the lines with collaborations are **Group Exchanges**. There are some sites or programs that you can pay to be a member of, where the members purposely swap quotes, interviews, guest blog post, etc.

This isn't the same as paying for links (which I'm strongly against). The purpose of these groups is just to connect people with sites that are also looking for links.

Smart Link Exchanges, you want to be careful about every site linking to you, you are linking back to it. Google likes to see people just organically linking to you, so when I'm working with clients, and when we're working in our mastermind, we form a linking triangle, or a linking square, where site one will link to site two, site two will link to site three, site three will link to site one. That way, everybody's got a link, but it doesn't make it look like we're all friends. You can do that in as big or little as you want to. Don't go and say, "Hey, let's exchange links." Try to just work with people to get a link.

As you can see from this list, the most important thing about getting backlinks is you have to reach out and ask for them.

It's a much slower process if you wait for links to land in your lap. This is what most sites do, and this is what's hurting their SEO the most.

I've been asking you to collect names of potential sites, and as we've been going through this chapter, use this list and the pitch templates on the resource site, **onlineboutiquesource.com/SEObookresources** and start reaching out to a minimum of 10 sources a week.

Some Dos and Don'ts of Backlinking

DO	DON'T
Create links within text (they get clicked more because people are already reading)	Spam links by just having a bunch of unrelated links everywhere
Put the best links on the top of your page	Comment on blogs, Reddit, or other forums to build links
	Buy Links

How do you know who's linking to you?

This is the last little piece about links. After you've done all the work to get links, you'll want to track who's linking to you and make sure that the links are good for your SEO. It's important to know that anyone can link to you, and while we do the work to get all of these great links, as your site's popularity grows, you may get links you don't recognize.

Three Sites to use to see who is linking to you (there will be a video on the resource site)

- Google Search Console
- AHREF
- Sem Rush

> **EXERCISE**
>
> Using a variety of the backlink strategies above create a list of people and sites you can pitch, also add 3 topics to pitch each site.
>
> This is an ongoing exercise; you'll see in the monthly plans a space to create a short pitch list east month.

Sites to Pitch for Backlinks				
Site Name	URL	Owner	Email	Social Handles
1				
Topics to Pitch Them				
2				
Topics to Pitch Them				
3				
Topics to Pitch Them				
4				
Topics to Pitch Them				
5				
Topics to Pitch Them				
6				
Topics to Pitch Them				
7				
Topics to Pitch Them				

The Ranking Checklist

2) **Initial site checks**
   - ✓ Confirm Google analytics access (Chapter 2)
   - ✓ Confirm Google search console (Chapter 2)
   - ✓ Get Current Metrics (Chapter 2)
   - ✓ Do initial site readiness checks (Chapter 4)
     - ✓ 404 errors
     - ✓ Address URL issues
     - ✓ Blank descriptions
     - ✓ Duplicate content
     - ✓ Broken links
     - ✓ Blank alt tags

3) **Complete keyword research (Chapter 5)**
   - ✓ Round Up- Create list of potential keywords
   - ✓ Analyze- Check volume and competition for keywords
   - ✓ Connect- Create a potential list of topics and categories
   - ✓ Engage- Test your words out in post and on social
   - ✓ Select 5-10 focus keywords

4) **Update Content on site**
   - ✓ Add keywords to pages on your site (Chapter 6)
   - ✓ Find Update images (Chapter 6)
   - ✓ Update page tags, descriptions, headings, images, etc. (Chapter 6)
   - ✓ Choose SEO friendly topics (Chapter 7)
   - ✓ Choose blog post types you like (Chapter 7)
   - ✓ Write 5-10 blog post (Chapter 7)

5) **Internal inks (Chapter 8)**
   - ✓ Identify pages without links
   - ✓ Identify pages to link to on your site
   - ✓ Create internal links

6) **External Linking (Chapter 8)**
   - ✓ Find link building opportunities
   - ✓ Fid group to collaborate with
   - ✓ Monitor incoming links

7) **Wrap up and ongoing (Chapter 9)**
   - ☐ Schedule future blog post
   - ☐ Pitch link building opportunities
   - ☐ Update target keywords
   - ☐ Complete Monthly Look back and plan ahead
   - ☐ Monthly 2-4 blog post with internal link
   - ☐ Monthly 5-10 backlinks

Chapter 9 Keep this same SEO Energy

There's a difference between knowing the path and walking the path- Morpheus, The Matrix

Now that we've gone through all the steps it takes to start, grow and build your SEO, I want to talk a little bit how to keep it up and what to do as you start getting your numbers. Putting SEO work into your regular practice is what keeps the SEO party going and traffic flowing. While SEO traffic isn't as volatile as Social media (if you stop posting, it stops growing), it can and will slowly diminish if you ignore it. There are planner and journal prompts right after this chapter, that will help you keep things going, and in this chapter, I'll talk about some things to consider to keep your SEO going, some frequently asked questions and 2019 trends to be on the lookout for.

When will I see results from my SEO work?

This is the hardest but most common question when you do SEO wok. The best answer is "it depends". It depends on your keywords, type of content, rate of backlinks, current ranking etc.; there are a lot of factors that go into when and how well you'll rank.

Butttt, you can't go and tell your boss or you bank it depends LOL. Instead of waiting around for rankings to happen I look for a few indicators that tell me if I'm on the right track or if I need to do something different with the work I've put in.

No one wants to spend months going down the wrong path, so I put together this quick chart to tell you the results you should look for to tell if it's all working.

And YES you should see movement in 30 days!!!

First 30 Days	60-90 days	120+ days
You should start seeing new keywords and keywords that are going up in the position in Google Search Console	You should start getting hits to some of those new pages and change pages that you've done	If you are seeing growth in the original set of keywords, you can focus on a new set of on your list.

How often do you need to post?

The frequency at which you post depends on where you are in your SEO journey

Getting Started: create 10 posts in 3 categories, put the first five posts up to start your blog and schedule out the other five posts weekly to post your first five weeks of content. Then continue for the first four or five months with a weekly or bi-weekly post. After the first few months, you can post as little as two times a month.

Existing site: Similar to a new site, create 10 posts around your new keywords in one category. Schedule the first five to post twice a week and the remaining five, weekly. After the initial post, post for the first four or five months weekly or bi-weekly. After the first few months, you can post as little as twice a month.

How often to get new links?

Links are just as important as putting up new content. You want to keep linking even after the initial SEO push. In the beginning, you want to get as many links as possible, shoot for at least 10 a week. After the first three months, you want to continue your growth with at least two to three new links per month. Remember, Google is always looking at your site, they're looking at how often you're updating content, how often you're getting links, and how you're raising your popularity levels.

Why do things and Ranks Change

The Effect of Algorithm Changes

We already know that Google changes. At the beginning of the book, I joked about when people scream about Google changing, the algorithm change, and all of the problems and issues that they may or may not be encountering from the changes. Just like everything else, the algorithms are going to change. Instead of being nervous about them, I want you to be prepared.

The SEO methods we've talked about here in this book will help you create content and build SEO naturally; the way search engines intend to find content. This is a very content-based method and more of listening to your customers and making sure that the content on your site is meeting the needs that people have in your niche. These methods have proven time and time again to be the most effective with the algorithm. Google's entire reason for being is to present people with the best possible search results, and when your site is in line with those goals, you'll do better than most when things changes.

Do SEO the way that Google wants it done and not trying to do any black hat, scammy tactics, such as buying links or creating frivolous content (which I did not teach you any spam in this book). You may hear about and see sites using these methods, and you'll wonder why you didn't learn about it here. The main reason is to ensure that when Google changes to clean up the scammers, I want your site to be the least impacted.

People Change more than the algorithm

We hear a lot talk about algorithm changes that I just discussed, but it's not just the algorithm that changes that will impact your SEO efforts; people change too.

Here's an example: A couple years ago, my husband was thinking of putting together an SEO-driven site. We looked at topics and keywords around electronic cigarettes (also known as vapes). At that time, some of the keywords for electronic cigarettes, e-cigs, and vapes were pretty low, and it was a pretty great time to create a vape site. But he didn't, and over time, people started putting up more sites, and people started searching for them differently. The competition for vapes has gone way up, and the search volumes for e-cigarettes and e-cig is really low because no one calls it that anymore. He could still build a site around these topics, but it wouldn't grow as quickly as it would have 2–3 years ago.

One of the things that's really important with SEO is to **keep your fingers on the pulse of your industry, and the pulse of what people are doing, saying, and how they're using language.** It's important to understand and keep an eye out on what your people are saying, how are they speaking.

When people start to change their language and change how they're labeling things in your industry, you can either update some of your current content to include some of the new languages, or you can create new content using the new languages. Sometimes, bridging the new language to the old, like we did in my Peplum top example I've talked about in chapter seven. So the important thing is that people change, and you want to make sure that the language that you're using stays up-to-date with the language that people are searching and speaking, so you are always talking how your potential searchers are going to talk.

Competition Changes

In the vape example above, you'll see that not only did the searches change but also, competition will improve. As topics and keywords get more popular, more people will write about it. Even if those writers aren't working on their SEO, their content with the right keywords could impact how your keywords rank too. This happened to me with Online Boutique Source. When I started talking about Online Boutiques, my KC number were in the 20s, but now, they are in the high 30s. More people started talking about boutiques and focusing on boutiques, and naturally, the competition has gotten better.

The good news is if you're one of the first to talk about a topic, Google is going to give you a little bit of leverage, but you'll also want to add new keywords and content to remain competitive. The frequency we talked about in earlier chapters becomes more important when you have a competitive keyword. This is also why we always do the monthly checks. You'll want to keep a pulse on where some of your numbers are going, and if you see competition creeping up, create more content and build more links to those keywords.

Using the monthly planner sheets will help you to recognize and navigate all of these changes. This is why we have our monthly look forward and look back; if you're tracking how existing keywords are doing, it'll be easier to see which you should focus on next.

Oh the Places you can SEO

LOL, I'm a big Dr. Seuss fan.

Next thing I want to talk about before we wrap up this book is other sites and platforms you can use your new SEO skill. Throughout this book, you've learned a really important skill that doesn't just work on your website and search engine platforms, but there are a lot of sites that case their search and algorithms on the same factors as the search engine.

Most platforms look at these things when they decide what content to show and what to hide

- What topics are people searching for?
- What topics and pages are people engaging with?
- Which pages and post consistently get a lot of engagement and enjoyment?

I use some of my same SEO skills and principle in just about every platform that I'm on. people always ask, "well, how do you get such good results on other sites if you don't do all the things the xyz experts say?" I don't do all the posting things. I don't do all the follow, no-follow things; I don't do all the things. The reasons I'm able to still get good results on platforms without doing all these things is because I use a lot of my same SEO practices and principles.

First, I use the same keywords across all of my platforms. So whether it's social media, YouTube, Pinterest, I always use some of the same keywords. If people are searching for it on Google, they're searching for it on YouTube, they're searching for on Pinterest, they're searching for it everywhere.

Second, I talk about the same topics that are performing well on my site or vice versa. If something's doing really well on my social media, I'll write something about it on my site. If something's doing really well on my site, I will write about it on my social media. This always gives me something to share that will get good engagement.

Third, I use social media for research. So I'm often giving social media back the same energy they are giving and answering the big questions they have right now. And you know, throughout this book, I've talked about using social media for a lot of my research. Sometimes if I'm answering a question in a group, I will answer it and then copy that answer over to my site and make it into some more content. That's really important.

SEO on YouTube

Google owns YouTube, so it has one of the closest related algorithms. That's really important and helpful to help you grow on two platforms at once. Also, videos from YouTube show up in their own section on the google search results page. You'll really want to make sure that you're optimizing your YouTube videos.

1) In the description of your video, use keywords and descriptive language about what's in the video. Watch other videos on related topics and see what are the top keywords that stand out for those videos. In the blurb, talk about the keywords and the top questions that are answered in the video.
2) If you have other related blog posts, link them in the blurb on YouTube. If I have a blog post that goes with this, or other blog posts that are related to the topic of my video, I will link those in my YouTube video links. They don't count as much as regular backlinks, but they do count a little bit, and it's always great to get people and traffic back to your site. So I will link anything that's relevant from my YouTube to my site, and I do not link YouTube to other YouTube videos. Our goal is traffic to your site, so all roads should lead to your site.
3) I also do a lot of embedding of my videos on the site. I even have a full video page, but you can embed your videos into a blog post as we talked about in chapter seven. Another good reason for embedding videos on my site is because that's going to get me double the benefit. When people watch on your site, Google is going to see that people spent longer on your site and YouTube is going to count it towards your video viewed time.

SEO on Pinterest

Pinterest is another one of my major SEO-friendly platforms. Pinterest is very search-friendly, and there are a few things you can do to enhance your Pinterest SEO.

1) I make sure that the images have the title on it. Pinterest is all about the image, but people still want to see what the pin is about before they click the link. Putting the title on the link encourages searchers to click through more. If you look at all my blog posts, all of the blog images have the title on it for Pinterest.
2) On Pinterest, I re-write the descriptions similar to YouTube, include keywords and a little about what the post is about. Usually, it's the same thing I put in the Meta description.
3) My Pinterest boards are set up around keywords. I'll put keywords in the board name and segment them, similar to the SEO categories I have on my site.

Pinterest has a really good algorithm that is very similar to Google, although it's not owned by Google. All of these steps help me to get much better results on Pinterest, and I don't have to do things like group boards. I don't pin every day like people talk about.

My 2019 SEO Predictions

Before we end the book, I wanted to share my look ahead at the state of SEO over the next year or so. Like all marketing channels, SEO is an ever-changing and growing landscape. I'm sure I'll update it with newer versions, or there'll be updates on the resource website, as the years go by. But if you're reading this in the 2018 – 2019 time frame, these are my predictions for what's coming up in search and how you can best set yourself up to handle them.

Prediction #1 – The Rise of Video Marketing

Video is going to be really, really big. More people are looking at video on social, which means they'll also be looking at video in search. As you know from reading this book, Google only reads texts, so it is going to be more and more important for you to make sure that you've got some texts around your videos and images too. Don't just become a vlogger and put up videos and don't say anything about what's in them.

The other thing about videos is to embed them on your site. You want to get people off YouTube and other platforms and onto your site as quickly as possible. So get good at embedding videos on your site.

Prediction #2 – No business is an island

My second prediction for the upcoming years is collaborations will be key. As more and more people are creating content, more and more people are getting out here and getting started with businesses, blogging, and just creating content. What's going to set you apart is going to be collaborating with other people and getting those links. Those links we already talked about are the secret sauce of SEO, and they are going to be like the mandatory sauce of SEO. A perfect site with no backlinks is going to get nowhere in search, because the only way Google's going to be able to tell the difference between your amazing information and the next person's amazing information is how popular this person's site is, compared to yours.

So collaborations and getting those backlinks are going to be the easiest ways. Yes, you can get backlinks without actually collaborating or talking to someone. But as I said in chapter eight, it's much easier to work with people you know, and it's a lot more predictable when you just talk to people that you know and that you're probably already talking to, working with and being around on social media.

Prediction #3 – Voice Search is a thing

The last prediction is the increase in the use of voice search. Voice search is when a person uses something like Siri or Alexa to search for something. So I've heard a lot about voice search in 2018, and I'm sure it's just going to continue to move because more people are using their mobile devices, home voice-activated and smart devices. With these, people will stop typing and start speaking more. You want to make sure to set yourself up to do well with voice search.

The way to make sure that you're set up is using as much natural language as possible. This may be anti-grammar Nazi, or you know, anti-perfect textbook English, but you want to make sure that when you're writing, you use a little bit more casual language and then get into the real technical stuff. You've even seen it in this book – talk to your audience like you would when you meet.

So those are my top three predictions moving forward. I hope you have enjoyed this book and feel more equipped to go after those rankings.

Don't forget to visit **OnlineBoutiqueSource.com/SEObookresources** to sign up for resources, videos and links referenced in the book, and if you need more SEO support along your journey, join us in the SEO WorkClub. That is the companion membership to go with this book, that will help you to really work with other people as you guys move forward in your SEO journey.

The next two sections of the book are your journal and planner pages.

There are 30 journal prompts based on a lot of what we've learned in chapter five and six. So, taking that and helping you to write, and look at writing naturally, write how you would write, don't overthink it, just answer the questions, or use the prompt to help you write out what would be your blog posts.

I give you a full page to start writing down what you want, or you can just write down ideas, and then put them in an actual blog post, but every prompt is a blog post. So, every prompt can easily be transferred right onto your site. Some of them, you can even do more than one time. So, you know, I'd say something like, "What's the last question someone asked you?" Do it three times. If you do that prompt thrice, that's three blog posts. The section after that is the planner section, and that is, as I mentioned earlier, the look back and look forward to help keep track of your numbers and to help map out what you're going to do in the month going forward.

Definitely use that. If you use that for the next 12 months, really, you have no choice but for your SEO to grow. So these are two really important parts I wanted to put into this book to make this book not only something that you learn a lot of SEO, which hopefully you got it now, but also something that is actually doing the SEO. So putting all those exercises that we've done together, putting all this research that we've done together and really start putting it into action, those planner pages are going to be what's key for you. Hope you've enjoyed the book, and I will see you guys in the search engines.

The Ranking Checklist

1) **Initial site checks**
   - ✓ Confirm Google analytics access (Chapter 2)
   - ✓ Confirm Google search console (Chapter 2)
   - ✓ Get Current Metrics (Chapter 2)
   - ✓ Do initial site readiness checks (Chapter 4)
     - ✓ 404 errors
     - ✓ Address URL issues
     - ✓ Blank descriptions
     - ✓ Duplicate content
     - ✓ Broken links
     - ✓ Blank alt tags

2) **Complete keyword research (Chapter 5)**
   - ✓ Round Up- Create list of potential keywords
   - ✓ Analyze- Check volume and competition for keywords
   - ✓ Connect- Create a potential list of topics and categories
   - ✓ Engage- Test your words out in post and on social
   - ✓ Select 5-10 focus keywords

3) **Update Content on site**
   - ✓ Add keywords to pages on your site (Chapter 6)
   - ✓ Find Update images (Chapter 6)
   - ✓ Update page tags, descriptions, headings, images, etc. (Chapter 6)
   - ✓ Choose SEO friendly topics (Chapter 7)
   - ✓ Choose blog post types you like (Chapter 7)
   - ✓ Write 5-10 blog post (Chapter 7)

4) **Internal inks (Chapter 8)**
   - ✓ Identify pages without links
   - ✓ Identify pages to link to on your site
   - ✓ Create internal links

5) **External Linking (Chapter 8)**
   - ✓ Find link building opportunities
   - ✓ Fid group to collaborate with
   - ✓ Monitor incoming links

6) **Wrap up and ongoing (Chapter 9)**
   - ✓ Schedule future blog post
   - ✓ Pitch link building opportunities
   - ✓ Update target keywords
   - ✓ Complete Monthly Look back and plan ahead
   - ✓ Monthly 2-4 blog post with internal link
   - ✓ Monthly 5-10 backlinks

The Journal Pages

What Are the Journal Pages About?

This journal section is one of the most important parts of the book to me.

We've learned a lot of what you should do for SEO in this book, but I know the actual doing is still a constant struggle. So I created prompts for you to go through 30 different questions to help you get this good content out of your head and onto your site.

You've probably heard my story about the Q&A box I used to help me with my first blog post with Online Boutique Source, that started getting thousands of visits in the first few months.

The best content often is the answer to someone's questions. Answering the right questions was critical to the SEO success of my site, so I've designed these pages to give you the most common questions that people search for.

This is your own little Q&A box. Answer these questions and prompts as if you were explaining to a potential customer who knows nothing about your business.

The best part is each prompt can be taken right from here and can become a post on your site. We covered the 7 blog post types in chapter 6, and that'll help you take these prompts from scattered thoughts in your head to your next top ranking post.

If you use 1 journal answer a week on your site, you'll have enough blog content for the next 7 and a half months.

So dive right in and start Writing

What is the last question someone asked you about your business? Explain the question and answer

My SEO Workbook

How does your service or product make your customer's life easier? list 3 reasons and explain

My SEQ Workbook

What are 3 things you need to know before getting started with product or service

[Hint writing list in odd numbers 3,5,7 are more inviting to readers. Often you'll see ask for things in 3, if you have more don't worry we can make it another post]

My SEO Workbook

What roadblocks does one face when getting started with your service or products

What helped you get started learning about your industry?

My SEO Workbook

What are 3 ways your product or service has helped you? (Tell your personal story)

What are 3 mistakes people make when starting or trying to DIY your product or service?

Who's a big name in your industry and what lessons have you learned from them?

Compare tools or common things in your Niche

Example: "Wrap dress Vs. Sheath Dress" or "Email Sales Funnel Vs. Messenger Bot Sales Funnel"

My SEO Workbook

Feature a top person, company, or celebrity industry

People love to hear success stories, and how other people are doing with a strategy or product, this lets them know its ok to try it

Tell your story and what you learned from it

This isn't just to talk about you but talk about how what you sell helped you and the lessons you learned from it

My SEO Workbook

Myth Buster Bust some myths that people think about your product or service

TIP: this could make for good email content too ☺

How to: Make it easy for them give people a step by step instructions on how to do something small in your niche. Example: "how to set up your first SB ad in ad manager."

My SEO Workbook

What is the last question someone asked you about your business? Explain the question and answer (check Facebook groups for questions)

My SEO Workbook

How does your service or product make your customers live easier list 3 reasons and explain?

My SEO Workbook

What are 3 things you need to know before getting started with your service or product

Top tools list 3-5 tools you use and explain (good place for affiliates

The future of… give an outlook of what your niche should look out for in 2019

My SEO Workbook

Lessons Learned from a trending topic. Pick a trending topic and give a few lessons you've learned or that people in your niche could learn from the event.

How they could have done better. Here's your chance to tell them how it is, find a trending topic or significant event in your niche and tell them things they could have done to avoid the situation or do it better (caution try to keep it positive, even criticism can be given nicely)

Here's an example http://onlineboutiquesource.com/shea-moistures-biggest-mistake-wasnt-just-made-yesterday

My SEO Workbook

Top stories/ tweets about a topic. Think buzz feed style. This is easy if you're short on time. Search twitter or google and compile some of the best responses of information about a trending topic

Give a book review? This is in honor of Mrs. O (LOL). Read or Listen to a new hot topic book and give your review about it, tie to your niche and what they should pay attention to. HINT this can be done for podcast, books, you get the idea.

Be a live event correspondent. This sounds really fancy, but it's a lot easier than you think, similar to the book review but this for a live one-time event. Think awards ceremony, conference, etc. Help your readers experience what they may have missed. [HINT Don't worry if you don't have time to leave the house this works well for events broadcast on TV too, think red carpets during award seasons, or the royal wedding thoughts ;)]

The Planner Pages

How to use the Planner pages?

Last part, are the monthly reviews. So even if you don't stay on track with everything I just said, like I said, there are 12 months of monthly reviews here at the end of the book in the planner section. Each monthly review is two pages. There's one page that I'm calling the look back and that is where you're going to record all of your stats month over month. So it's all of the things we've talked about that you should be looking at in Google search console, and Google analytics.

Month 1 Check

The Look Back- How did you do last month

	Week 1	Week 2	Week 3	Week 4
Page Visits Total				
Page Visits from Google				
Bounce Rate				
Average Time on Site				
Keywords Ranking				
Keywords 1-10				
Backlinks				

Top Pages visited	
1	
2	
3	

Top Pages ranking	
1	
2	
3	

Top Keywords by Position	Top Keywords by Impression	Top Keywords by Click Through Rate

What was my big Ranking Win this month?	What Can I do more of next month?

Month 1 Check

The Plan Ahead- What are our plans for this month

R.A.C.E. Focus Keywords

	Keyword	Volume	Competition Score	Category	Related Product/Service
1					
2					
3					
4					
5					

Blog post to write this month

	Topic	Blog Type	Links to other content
1			
2			
3			
4			
5			

Sites to Pitch for Backlinks

	Site Name	URL	Owner	Email	Social Handles
1					
	Topics to Pitch Them				
2					
	Topics to Pitch Them				
3					
	Topics to Pitch Them				
4					
	Topics to Pitch Them				

Month 2 Check

The Look Back- How did you do last month

	Week 1	Week 2	Week 3	Week 4
Page Visits Total				
Page Visits from Google				
Bounce Rate				
Average Time on Site				
Keywords Ranking				
Keywords 1-10				
Backlinks				

Top Pages visited	
1	
2	
3	

Top Pages ranking	
1	
2	
3	

Top Keywords by Position	Top Keywords by Impression	Top Keywords by Click Through Rate

What was my big Ranking Win this month?	What Can I do more of next month?

Month 2 Check

The Plan Ahead - What are our plans for this month

R.A.C.E. Focus Keywords				
	Keyword	Volume	Competition Score	Category	Related Product/Service
1					
2					
3					
4					
5					

Blog post to write this month			
	Topic	Blog Type	Links to other content
1			
2			
3			
4			
5			

Sites to Pitch for Backlinks					
	Site Name	URL	Owner	Email	Social Handles
1					
	Topics to Pitch Them				
2					
	Topics to Pitch Them				
3					
	Topics to Pitch Them				
4					
	Topics to Pitch Them				

Month 3 Check

The Look Back - How did you do last month

	Week 1	Week 2	Week 3	Week 4
Page Visits Total				
Page Visits from Google				
Bounce Rate				
Average Time on Site				
Keywords Ranking				
Keywords 1-10				
Backlinks				

Top Pages visited	
1	
2	
3	

Top Pages ranking	
1	
2	
3	

Top Keywords by Position	Top Keywords by Impression	Top Keywords by Click Through Rate

What was my big Ranking Win this month?	What Can I do more of next month?

Month 3 Check

The Plan Ahead- What are our plans for this month

R.A.C.E. Focus Keywords				
Keyword	Volume	Competition Score	Category	Related Product/Service
1				
2				
3				
4				
5				

Blog post to write this month		
Topic	Blog Type	Links to other content
1		
2		
3		
4		
5		

Sites to Pitch for Backlinks				
Site Name	URL	Owner	Email	Social Handles
1				
Topics to Pitch Them				
2				
Topics to Pitch Them				
3				
Topics to Pitch Them				
4				
Topics to Pitch Them				

Month 4 Check

The Look Back- How did you do last month

	Week 1	Week 2	Week 3	Week 4
Page Visits Total				
Page Visits from Google				
Bounce Rate				
Average Time on Site				
Keywords Ranking				
Keywords 1-10				
Backlinks				

Top Pages visited	
1	
2	
3	

Top Pages ranking	
1	
2	
3	

Top Keywords by Position	Top Keywords by Impression	Top Keywords by Click Through Rate

What was my big Ranking Win this month?	What Can I do more of next month?

Month 4 Check

The Plan Ahead- What are our plans for this month

R.A.C.E. Focus Keywords				
Keyword	Volume	Competition Score	Category	Related Product/Service
1				
2				
3				
4				
5				

Blog post to write this month		
Topic	Blog Type	Links to other content
1		
2		
3		
4		
5		

Sites to Pitch for Backlinks				
Site Name	URL	Owner	Email	Social Handles
1				
Topics to Pitch Them				
2				
Topics to Pitch Them				
3				
Topics to Pitch Them				
4				
Topics to Pitch Them				

Month 5 Check

The Look Back - How did you do last month

	Week 1	Week 2	Week 3	Week 4
Page Visits Total				
Page Visits from Google				
Bounce Rate				
Average Time on Site				
Keywords Ranking				
Keywords 1-10				
Backlinks				

Top Pages visited	
1	
2	
3	

Top Pages ranking	
1	
2	
3	

Top Keywords by Position	Top Keywords by Impression	Top Keywords by Click Through Rate

What was my big Ranking Win this month?	What Can I do more of next month?

Month 5 Check
The Plan Ahead- What are our plans for this month

R.A.C.E. Focus Keywords				
	Keyword	Volume	Competition Score	Category	Related Product/Service
1					
2					
3					
4					
5					

Blog post to write this month			
	Topic	Blog Type	Links to other content
1			
2			
3			
4			
5			

Sites to Pitch for Backlinks					
	Site Name	URL	Owner	Email	Social Handles
1					
	Topics to Pitch Them				
2					
	Topics to Pitch Them				
3					
	Topics to Pitch Them				
4					
	Topics to Pitch Them				

Month 6 Check
The Look Back- How did you do last month

	Week 1	Week 2	Week 3	Week 4
Page Visits Total				
Page Visits from Google				
Bounce Rate				
Average Time on Site				
Keywords Ranking				
Keywords 1-10				
Backlinks				

Top Pages visited	
1	
2	
3	

Top Pages ranking	
1	
2	
3	

Top Keywords by Position	Top Keywords by Impression	Top Keywords by Click Through Rate

What was my big Ranking Win this month?	What Can I do more of next month?

Month 6 Check

The Plan Ahead- What are our plans for this month

R.A.C.E. Focus Keywords				
Keyword	Volume	Competition Score	Category	Related Product/Service
1				
2				
3				
4				
5				

Blog post to write this month		
Topic	Blog Type	Links to other content
1		
2		
3		
4		
5		

Sites to Pitch for Backlinks				
Site Name	URL	Owner	Email	Social Handles
1				
Topics to Pitch Them				
2				
Topics to Pitch Them				
3				
Topics to Pitch Them				
4				
Topics to Pitch Them				

Month 7 Check

The Look Back - How did you do last month

	Week 1	Week 2	Week 3	Week 4
Page Visits Total				
Page Visits from Google				
Bounce Rate				
Average Time on Site				
Keywords Ranking				
Keywords 1-10				
Backlinks				

Top Pages visited	
1	
2	
3	

Top Pages ranking	
1	
2	
3	

Top Keywords by Position	Top Keywords by Impression	Top Keywords by Click Through Rate

What was my big Ranking Win this month?	What Can I do more of next month?

Month 7 Check
The Plan Ahead- What are our plans for this month

R.A.C.E. Focus Keywords				
Keyword	Volume	Competition Score	Category	Related Product/Service
1				
2				
3				
4				
5				

Blog post to write this month		
Topic	Blog Type	Links to other content
1		
2		
3		
4		
5		

Sites to Pitch for Backlinks				
Site Name	URL	Owner	Email	Social Handles
1				
Topics to Pitch Them				
2				
Topics to Pitch Them				
3				
Topics to Pitch Them				
4				
Topics to Pitch Them				

Month 8 Check

The Look Back- How did you do last month

	Week 1	Week 2	Week 3	Week 4
Page Visits Total				
Page Visits from Google				
Bounce Rate				
Average Time on Site				
Keywords Ranking				
Keywords 1-10				
Backlinks				

Top Pages visited	
1	
2	
3	

Top Pages ranking	
1	
2	
3	

Top Keywords by Position	Top Keywords by Impression	Top Keywords by Click Through Rate

What was my big Ranking Win this month?	What Can I do more of next month?

Month 8 Check

The Plan Ahead- What are our plans for this month

R.A.C.E. Focus Keywords				
	Keyword	Volume	Competition Score	Category	Related Product/Service
1					
2					
3					
4					
5					

Blog post to write this month		
	Topic	Blog Type	Links to other content
1			
2			
3			
4			
5			

Sites to Pitch for Backlinks				
	Site Name	URL	Owner	Email	Social Handles
1					
	Topics to Pitch Them				
2					
	Topics to Pitch Them				
3					
	Topics to Pitch Them				
4					
	Topics to Pitch Them				

Month 9 Check

The Look Back- How did you do last month

	Week 1	Week 2	Week 3	Week 4
Page Visits Total				
Page Visits from Google				
Bounce Rate				
Average Time on Site				
Keywords Ranking				
Keywords 1-10				
Backlinks				

Top Pages visited	
1	
2	
3	

Top Pages ranking	
1	
2	
3	

Top Keywords by Position	Top Keywords by Impression	Top Keywords by Click Through Rate

What was my big Ranking Win this month?	What Can I do more of next month?

Month 9 Check

The Plan Ahead- What are our plans for this month

R.A.C.E. Focus Keywords				
	Keyword	Volume	Competition Score	Category	Related Product/Service
1					
2					
3					
4					
5					

Blog post to write this month			
	Topic	Blog Type	Links to other content
1			
2			
3			
4			
5			

Sites to Pitch for Backlinks					
	Site Name	URL	Owner	Email	Social Handles
1					
	Topics to Pitch Them				
2					
	Topics to Pitch Them				
3					
	Topics to Pitch Them				
4					
	Topics to Pitch Them				

My SEO Workbook

Month 10 Check

The Look Back - How did you do last month

	Week 1	Week 2	Week 3	Week 4
Page Visits Total				
Page Visits from Google				
Bounce Rate				
Average Time on Site				
Keywords Ranking				
Keywords 1-10				
Backlinks				

Top Pages visited	
1	
2	
3	

Top Pages ranking	
1	
2	
3	

Top Keywords by Position	Top Keywords by Impression	Top Keywords by Click Through Rate

What was my big Ranking Win this month?	What Can I do more of next month?

Month 10 Check

The Plan Ahead- What are our plans for this month

R.A.C.E. Focus Keywords				
	Keyword	Volume	Competition Score	Category	Related Product/Service
1					
2					
3					
4					
5					

Blog post to write this month			
	Topic	Blog Type	Links to other content
1			
2			
3			
4			
5			

Sites to Pitch for Backlinks					
	Site Name	URL	Owner	Email	Social Handles
1					
	Topics to Pitch Them				
2					
	Topics to Pitch Them				
3					
	Topics to Pitch Them				
4					
	Topics to Pitch Them				

Month 11 Check

The Look Back- How did you do last month

	Week 1	Week 2	Week 3	Week 4
Page Visits Total				
Page Visits from Google				
Bounce Rate				
Average Time on Site				
Keywords Ranking				
Keywords 1-10				
Backlinks				

Top Pages visited	
1	
2	
3	

Top Pages ranking	
1	
2	
3	

Top Keywords by Position	Top Keywords by Impression	Top Keywords by Click Through Rate

What was my big Ranking Win this month?	What Can I do more of next month?

Month 11 Check

The Plan Ahead- What are our plans for this month

R.A.C.E. Focus Keywords				
Keyword	Volume	Competition Score	Category	Related Product/Service
1				
2				
3				
4				
5				

Blog post to write this month		
Topic	Blog Type	Links to other content
1		
2		
3		
4		
5		

Sites to Pitch for Backlinks				
Site Name	URL	Owner	Email	Social Handles
1				
Topics to Pitch Them				
2				
Topics to Pitch Them				
3				
Topics to Pitch Them				
4				
Topics to Pitch Them				

Month 12 Check

The Look Back- How did you do last month

	Week 1	Week 2	Week 3	Week 4
Page Visits Total				
Page Visits from Google				
Bounce Rate				
Average Time on Site				
Keywords Ranking				
Keywords 1-10				
Backlinks				

Top Pages visited	
1	
2	
3	

Top Pages ranking	
1	
2	
3	

Top Keywords by Position	Top Keywords by Impression	Top Keywords by Click Through Rate

What was my big Ranking Win this month?	What Can I do more of next month?

Month 12 Check

The Plan Ahead- What are our plans for this month

R.A.C.E. Focus Keywords				
Keyword	Volume	Competition Score	Category	Related Product/Service
1				
2				
3				
4				
5				

Blog post to write this month		
Topic	Blog Type	Links to other content
1		
2		
3		
4		
5		

Sites to Pitch for Backlinks				
Site Name	URL	Owner	Email	Social Handles
1				
Topics to Pitch Them				
2				
Topics to Pitch Them				
3				
Topics to Pitch Them				
4				
Topics to Pitch Them				

Notes

Notes

Notes

Notes

Notes

Notes

Notes

Notes

Notes

Notes

Notes

Made in the USA
Middletown, DE
28 February 2019